FOREX TRADING

THE ULTIMATE GUIDE TO LEARN STRATEGIES, TOOLS, SECRETS AND FOREX TRADING PSYCHOLOGY

outlays.

By

Clarke Meadows

Copyright © 2019. All Rights Reserved.

This document is geared towards providing exact and reliable information concerning the topic and issue covered. The publication is sold with the idea that the publisher is not required to render accounting, officially permitted or otherwise qualified services. If advice is necessary, legal or professional, a practiced individual in the profession should be ordered.

- From a Declaration of Principles which was accepted and approved equally by a Committee of the American Bar Association and a Committee of Publishers and Associations.

In no way is it legal to reproduce, duplicate, or transmit any part of this document in either electronic means or printed format. Recording of this publication is strictly prohibited, and any storage of this document is not allowed unless with written permission from the publisher. All rights reserved.

The information provided herein is stated to be truthful and consistent, in that any liability, in terms of inattention or otherwise, by any usage or abuse of any policies, processes, or directions contained within is the sole and utter responsibility of the recipient reader. Under no circumstances will any legal obligation or blame be held against the publisher for any reparation, damages, or monetary loss due to the information herein, either directly or indirectly.

Respective authors own all copyrights not held by the publisher.

The information herein is offered for informational purposes solely and is universal as so. The presentation of the data is without a contract or any guarantee assurance.

The trademarks that are used are without any consent, and the publication of the logo is without permission or backing by the trademark owner. All trademarks and brands within this book are for clarifying purposes only and are owned by the owners themselves, not affiliated with this document

TABLE OF CONTENTS

Introduction 5
What Is Forex Trading... 9
Forex Market Hours And Trading Sessions 21
Choosing A Broker And Avoiding Forex Trading Fraud 30
Risk Management (Forex)... 38
Forex Trading Psychology 49
Forex Fundamental And Technical Analysis 54
Forex Order Types.. 64
Tips For Choosing Reliable Forex Trade Brokers 69
Short Term Forex Vs. Long Term Forex Trading....................... 77
Best Automated Forex Trading Software 89
What Are Forex Automated Trading Signals And Which Are The Best? 96
Why You Have To Start Forex Trading 106
Understanding Forex Market Analysis..................................... 111
What Is Stop-Loss In Forex Trading? 119
Forex Trading Benefits.. 127
Questions About Currency Trading.. 134
Conclusion.. 140
Do Not Go Yet; One Last Thing To Do 141

INTRODUCTION

If you are reading this book, kin interests you've got for Forex Trading are here to help everyone who has an interest in becoming a Forex trader. I have put together a series of guides that will walk you through the whole process. You probably have already got a basic understanding of however currency exchange rates will and do fluctuate but the means during which you're getting to be able to take advantage of being a

A forex trader can differ fully from; however, you will suppose you will be trading currencies!

Forex Market is a very exciting place. The only good thing about entering the forex market is that you can trade for your convenience at any time.

The world's largest foreign exchange market(' FX," Forex' or' FOREX') is measured by a daily turnover of more than US$ 5 trillion a day, which overshadows the combined turnover of the world's stock and bond markets. The forex market measuring propulsive turnover is one of many reasons why so many private investors and individual traders have entered the market. Investors have discovered several advantages, many of which are not available in other markets.

Forex is a coat of arms of foreign currency and exchange. Foreign exchange is a process of change from one currency to another for a variety of reasons, usually for trade, trade, or tourism. The Bank for International Settlements (the global central bank for domestic central banks) reported a recent three-year report that average daily forex trading volumes were over $5.1 trillion.

The exchange market, commonly known as Forex or just FX, is the largest financial market for purchasing, selling, and exchanging currencies. Instead of centralized bourses and transactions-that are the bondholders, through a global network of banks, brokers, and other financial institutions-they trade with each other in contrast, for example.

Forex is open 24 hours a day, five days a week, as a global market. Located in almost each time area–London, N York, Tokyo, Zurich, Frankfurt, Hong Kong, Singapore, Paris, and Sydney–major financial centers are located.

Depending on the exchange that is active during a specific time, there are three trading sessions: Asian, European and American

The price in foreign currencies indicates the quantity of the quotes (second) to be bought or sold for one unit of basis (first) and the amount to be bought or sold.

Currency value usually rises if demand is greater than supply, and if demand is smaller than supply, exchange rates are driven by supply and demand strengths. Prices also fluctuate as a result of economic, social and political events during the 24-hour day of trading.

Currency prices are also strongly affected by the political and economic performance of the countries concerned. For instance, in a country with a lower inflation rate, the currency value of its trading partners will typically rise relative to the currencies. Inflation is also strongly linked to the central bank's interest rate: lower interest rates can devalue the rate and vice versa.

Another harmful factor in price setting is orders from Forex market participants, which are quite diverse in their volume and influence.

The most volumes and the strongest influence on exchange rates are that of Governments and central banks, such as the European Central Bank, Bank of England, and the US Federal Reserve. Central banks are trying to control inflation, money supply, interest rates and they are responsible for overseeing commercial banking systems. They can use foreign exchange reserves to intervene in the market to stabilize currencies or achieve a particular economic goal.

The second largest group consists of major banks and bank associations, which form the so-called interbank market, through which they deal with each other and determine the currency prices observed by individual traders on the trading platform. Because forex is a decentralized market, you can often see that different banks offer slightly different exchange rates for the same currency. OctaFX customers receive the best bid / ask prices quoted from our vast liquidity pool.

Another group of foreign exchange participants is brokerage companies, which intermediate between individual traders and the market. They use Electronic Communications Networks, which can include various financial institutions, to offset orders from customers with their liquidity providers. This model eliminates conflicts of interest when an order is executed between the brokerage and its customer. An ECN brokerage is compensated, unlike a market maker, by a commission which can be either charged per order or included as markup in the distribution process

ECN courier provides the individual traders with access to the forex market, which was originally only the domain of big banks and profits from price fluctuations. Although the price fluctuations are small every day, the use of leverage may increase the value of these movements, often by less than 1 percent.

Traders interact with a courier via a trading platform-a soapstone that enables currencies to be purchased and sold. It can be installed or even accessed via a web browser on your desktop computer, mobile device.

WHAT IS FOREX TRADING

"Forex" means foreign exchange and refers, in exchange, to the purchase or sale of one currency. It is the largest traded market in the world because it has the participation of people, companies, and countries. You are participating in the global foreign exchange market when you go on a tour and translate your US dollars into euros.

Every day in a currency exchange market called Forex, millions of trades are produced. The term "Forex" begins straight with two phrases-" foreign "and" exchange. In contrast to other trading systems like the stock market, Forex does not involve physical or formal trading in goods. Instead, Forex works across currencies through purchasing, selling, and trading from different economies around the globe. Since the Forex market is truly a worldwide trading scheme, trading takes place 24 hours a day, five days a week. Moreover, no single control agency binds Forex, which implies Forex is the only real free-market financial trading scheme accessible today. By leaving exchange prices out of the hands of any group, even attempting to manipulate or corner the monetary market is much harder. With all the benefits of the Forex scheme and the worldwide involvement spectrum, the Forex market is the world's biggest market. Every day on the Forex market, between 1 trillion and 1.5 trillion equivalent U.S. dollars are traded.

Forex works primarily on the notion of "free-floating" currencies; this can best be described as currencies not supported by specific products such as gold or silver. Before 1971, a company like Forex would not function because of the worldwide "Bretton Woods" agreement. This preparation indicated that every country concerned would work to retain their currency value near the value of the US dollar, which was reserved at the gold value in turn. The Bretton Woods agreement of 1971 has been canceled. During the Vietnam conflict, the United States had run an enormous deficit and started printing more paper currency than gold could, leading to a comparatively elevated rate of inflation. By 1976, the scheme developed under the Bretton Woods Agreement had been deserted by every significant currency in the world and switched to a free-floating currency scheme. This free-floating scheme meant that the currency of each country could have very distinct fluctuating features depending on how the economy of the country at the moment was faring.

Some of the world's richest individuals have Forex as a major portion of their inventory of investments. Warren Buffet, the richest man in the world, has invested more than $20 trillion in the Forex sector in different currencies. His range of revenues generally includes well over one hundred million USD in every quartile profit from Forex trading.

George Soros is another big name in the currency trading industry-it is believed that he produced more than $1 billion in profit from a single trading day in 1992! Although these types of trades are very rare, he was still willing to accumulate more than $7 trillion from three decades of trading on the Forex market. George Soros' approach also shows that you don't have to be too dangerous to generate income on Forex — his liberal strategy involves removing large portions of its income from the industry, although the pattern of its various assets still seems to correlate upwards.

Keeping Your Emotions Out of Your Forex Trading

When you start in Forex, the biggest difficulty you'll encounter is not finding the finest Forex broker or the most profitable Forex trading scheme. Forex markets don't conspire against you, and you don't need some type of hidden knowledge of the industry to thrive. It may look like a cliche, but the biggest obstacle between you and the Forex profits you think of is your emotions.

What Systems Can And Can't Do For You

Don't catch me confused. You definitely need a good Forex broker and a profitable Forex trading system to trade Forex efficiently when you begin forex trading. That said, there are tens of great Forex brokers out there, and there are quite a few rewarding Forex trading systems out there, but very few people still manage to get away in Forex. Why? Because when trading, they don't regulate their feelings.

Two essential elements of effective Forex trading are emotional self-control and proper decision making. If you can handle your feelings soon on, trading a handbook scheme like a pro will be no issue. That said, if you recognize that you have problems regulating your emotions before, during, or after a trade, then you must be honest with yourself and confine yourself to instant Forex trading schemes until you're ready.

Automatic Forex trading systems will help you separate your emotions from trading as you learn how to manage them, as your scheme will make all your decisions.

Once you have your proven trading scheme in location, you are willing to start your Forex trading operation, but you are not yet plunging all of your available resources into your trading scheme. One of the traps falling into most people starting up in Forex is that they become greedy and risk all their hard-earned capital when they don't really know how to trade Forex with a system yet. They're just inexperienced with the system and are probable to create beginner mistakes at this point.

You should focus on learning how to trade Forex when you start in Forex instead of making loads of cash with Forex. That's supposed to happen afterward, after collecting Forex trading knowledge for at least a few months. You're trying to want to invest the minimum amount you need to trade in your plan while you start in Forex, and not more. Why? Because there's still a lot, you don't understand how to trade Forex, so you'll want to minimize your valuable assets while still having enough investment to care about what's going on.

Most people beginning out in Forex require a year or two to master their emotions fully, so there's nothing incorrect with running an instant Forex trading scheme to profit while studying. Indeed, to generate a business that maximizes their income while minimizing their hazards, many qualified traders trade a combination of manual and automated schemes.

What I propose to begin within Forex is, to be honest about your plan and your aspirations. Do not go into manual trading when you're not ready and remember that if you don't want to, you don't have to trade it yourself. You don't have to use a lucrative Forex trading scheme, and you may find you have a knack to construct Forex portfolios to increase your returns further, eliminating your business emotions entirely.

Thad B. is a qualified trading scheme developer who, for a private investment company, has developed and managed dozens of lucrative trading systems over the years. Forex trading systems are his hobby and expertise, and he has a bunch of helpful resources for any serious Forex system trader.

Luckily, to make a profit on Forex, you don't have to invest millions of bucks.

Many individuals have reported their achievement from $10,000 to as little as $100 for an original grant with original funds from anywhere. This broad range of economic requirements allows Forex an appealing location for all types to trade, from those well-established in the reduced rungs of the middle class to the world's richest individuals. Access to the Forex market is a relatively latest growth for those at the lesser end of the spectrum. Over the previous decades, different businesses have started delivering a scheme that is more compassionate to the average person, enabling the decreased original yields and higher effectiveness seen in today's industry. Now you can get began in whatever financial situation you are in.

While you can move directly into and start saving, it is important to create sure you get a stronger understanding of Forex trading ins and outs before you start.

The Forex workplace can be both profitable and pleasant, but understanding how the scheme operates to create a Forex job for you is crucial. You need a ton of practice to become a Forex pro, as with most lucrative activities. Precisely this, the mock exercise of Foreign Exchange, is offered by many blogs.

A Story Of Two Forex Traders Just Starting Out

Let me explain further with a story about two Forex traders: Tom and Jim have recently read a bunch about Forex. Both wasted internet hours trying to understand what currency trading is and how (and if) they can create some profits quickly. All the marketing ads they write inform you can increase your money very, very quickly. There is a danger engaged, of course, but it is just too nice to take on the future benefits. So they both decide to try Forex and see if they can.

Both kids are highly motivated and want to produce Forex with their biggest chance. So each of them is going to invest $1000 from their money in currency trading. They'll leave Forex if they lose the $1000 and re-evaluate whether to attempt again or not. Both demonstrated their dedication to creating Forex work for them by investing a thousand bucks.

Starting: Tom is taking all his $1000 and transferring it to an internet retail Forex broker. Tom will create all his commercial decisions on his own. He will be doing his research and sleeping on Forex forums and blogs to see if he will be able to get some much-needed advice.

Jim's trying a clear route. Even though he's just as driven as Tom, he's also aware of the complexity of the Forex market and understands that he doesn't have much knowledge at this point. So he is taking $900 and transferring it to the same Tom Forex broker wholesale. He spends the extra $100 to help him generate good company in an attempt to obtain entry to tools and assets (i.e., Forex trading systems and applications). Daily, he used to trade stocks, and he knows first-hand the advantage these tools and funds can have (especially if you know the strings).

Month 1: Tom immediately leaped into currency trading. His first trade started in the negative, but he quickly went west. He had wasted $100 before he was able to publish his selling request. Despite having some tiny profitable trades, his trading background was usually very similar to his first trading. Many trades started well, but he would eventually go down for some reason (he didn't have the knowledge or knowledge to understand). Tom's trading register was down to $400 at the close of his first month of trading currencies.

Jim, walked through some studies and discovered Forex with Ambush. This was an affiliation page that sends its workers hints. What captured his eye was that their trade messages were 99.9 percent accurate. How can they create such a courageous declaration? Jim pulled a little bit more and found a ton of positive feedback from the current staff. And there was one more item that eventually affected Jim to try Forex Ambush: at a percentage of their normal price, they are given a 7-day test.

Jim had seven days to check out Forex Ambush for less than twenty bucks and their 99.9 percent accurate trade messages. He's been enthusiastic about it. He had $900 in his Forex trading register, and he still had $80+ to use in event Forex Ambush did not help.

- ✓ Jim received an email from Forex Ambush with a trading message the following day. He was still very fresh to Forex, but as the trading message stipulated with the courageous precision declaration still in mind, Jim placed it in his command. Jim had made a profit of $145 earlier that day when his business was finished. He was excited! After his 7-day court was over, Jim went forward and signed up to be a continuous part of Forex

Ambush. Although not every trading message yielded profits, almost all of them were done. And he's had very small casualties. After one month, Jim had $1750 in his Forex trading register.

Month 2: Tom was feeling deflated. Within a month, he had gone from $1000 to $400. He made more valued, much more hazardous trades to try to return his money. The final outcome: he was down to $0 before the month ended. Tom was annoyed and angry. He signed off again doing Forex, saying it was a scam to anyone who would hear and save their cash.

Jim was nine in the cloud, on the other hand. The $900 he first got was changed to $1750. He still received a frequent email with trade clues from Forex Ambush, but he also inspected several other Forex trading systems. He had a much higher understanding of the Forex market after a month of lucrative trades and was complete of trust. Jim's trading proposal stood at $2355 at the beginning of month 2.

And the most noteworthy thing was that in his spare time, Jim was doing all this. To compensate for his travel costs, he still had a full-time job. Everything he did in Forex was extra. He regarded quitting his work on a full-time basis and trading Forex. But he's pleased for now with the stability his present work provides him and enjoys the advantages his "side" Forex cash is giving him.

Moral of the story: if you want to excel in anything you have very little knowledge and experience with, it is highly recommended that you spend in the tools and funds to increase your opportunities of accomplishment.

You must tell yourself: want to be like Tom, needy, upset, and swear that Forex is just a scam? Or would you love to spend in tools to help you perform and appreciate the income these tools will help you create? If you're severe about creating Forex money, then it's up to you to find a Forex trading system that will give you the gaining advantage.

A little healthy trepidation serves investors well. Active trading strategies and complex investment products don't have a place in most portfolios.

But maybe you have that balanced portfolio in place, and now you're looking for an adventure with some extra cash. Provided you know what you're doing — please take those words to heart — forex trading can be lucrative, and it requires a limited initial investment.

Trading Forex Is Different From Stock Trading In Several Ways:

- ✓ Forex trades are made over the counter — trader to trader or through forex brokers or dealers — rather than through a central exchange.
- ✓ Because traders work across time zones, the forex market is open 24 hours a day, five days a week.
- ✓ Currencies are always traded in pairs, and prices are quoted in pairs.
- ✓ Currency prices fluctuate rapidly but in small increments, which makes it hard for investors to make money on small trades. That's why currencies almost always are traded with leverage or money borrowed from the broker.

Since Forex is traded in pairs, it is always the same thing you exchange from currency to currency–buying one, selling another. The "majors" are 7 currencies, the euro (EUR), the United States (USD), Canadian (CAD), British (GBP), Australian (AUD), Japanese Yen (JPY), and Swiss (CHF) currencies, which are mostly traded: These currencies, combined with the US dollar, constitute the "major pairs."

What Is The Forex Market?

Currencies are traded on the foreign exchange market. The majority of people around the world have important foreign exchange currencies, whether or not they realize this, because foreign exchange and trade must be exchanged. If you live in the U.S., you or the company you buy from must pay the French for the cheese in Euros (EUR) if you are purchasing cheese from France. This means that the US importer should exchange U.S. dollars' (USD) equivalent value for euros. The same is true for the journey. In Egypt, a French tourist can not pay for the pyramids in euros, as this is not the currency locally accepted. In this respect, the tourist must exchange EUR for the local currency at the current exchange rate, in this case, the Egyptian pound.

The fact that there is no central exchange market is one of the only aspects of this world market. Rather, electronically, currency trading (OTCs) occurs via computer networks between traders all over the world and does not take place on centralized exchanges. The market has been open 24 hours a day, 5 and 1/2 days a week, and currencies traded throughout the world in major financial centers, including London, New York, Tokyo, and Zurich. This means that the market for forex starts in Tokyo and Hong Kong when the US trade day ends. As such, the market for forex can be very active every day with constantly changing prices.

To keep things ordered, most providers split pairs into the following categories:

- ✓ Major pairs - seven currencies that makeup 80% of global forex trading. Includes EUR/USD, USD/JPY, GBP/USD and USD/CHF
- ✓ Minor pairs - less frequently traded, these often feature major currencies against each other instead of the US dollar. Includes: EUR/GBP, EUR/CHF, GBP/JPY
- ✓ Exotics - a major currency against one from a small or emerging economy. Includes: USD/PLN, GBP/MXN, EUR/CZK
- ✓ Regional pairs - pairs classified by region – such as Scandinavia or Australasia. Includes: EUR/NOK, AUD/NZD, AUD/SGD

Most forex transactions are carried out by banks or individuals by seeking to buy a currency that will increase in value against the currency they sell. However, if you have ever converted one currency into another, for example, when traveling, you have made a forex transaction.

Understanding forex lot sizes

The "lot trades, forex." A micro lot is 1,000 units of currency, a mini lot is 10,000 units, and a standard lot is 100,000 units. The larger the lot size, the more risk you're taking on; individual investors should rarely trade standard lots.

We recommend that you stay on the micro lot while you are a beginner.

And hey, it seems to be a good place to notice that reputable forex brokers give investors almost always access to a demonstration trading account.

It's much more fun to lose play money than real money, especially while you're learning the ropes.

To help anyone concerned about becoming a Forex trader who developed a sequence of tips to direct you through the entire phase. You likely already have a fundamental knowledge of how currency exchange rates can fluctuate, but how you can benefit from being a Forex trader will be different from how you might believe you're trading currencies!

FOREX MARKET HOURS AND TRADING SESSIONS

It is generally assumed that the forex market is accessible 24 hours a day and seven days a week. The world competition for Forex is, in theory, accessible 24 hours seven days a week, but the hours a person can trad are still restricted. In comparison with other regulated markets, like the stock exchange, the Forex market consists of a network of financial institutions and retail traders that enables them to establish their operating hours. Operating forex hours are in line with their time zone. Most institutions trade between 8 a.m. At 4:00 p.m. Their local time zone is comparative.

Forex market is on record 24 hours a day and 5 1/2 days a week accessible for trading. It should also be observed that most experienced day traders realize that when business participation is strong during the operating hours, lucrative businesses occur. In other phrases, you can trade every day, early in the evening, but because of regular exercise, it might not simply be the most advantageous moment.

Many specialists recommend that the three biggest monetary business places, including London, New York, and Tokyo, should focus their business hours. You can use the highest business operation and the biggest chance of success in your regular Forex business by attacking these three main economies. Market professionals also indicate that when these significant market centers are also accessible, the most severe forex traders specifically aim and do their company. This short gap in business time areas leads to the most effective trading moments.

With weekly volumes of around $23 trillion, the Forex market is the world's biggest financial market. One must research all significant elements of the stock sector closely to become a good Forex Trader. These include Forex (FX) hours of trading and trading. When referring to the FX hours, what do we imply? They are the time's FX respondents who can buy, swap, and speculate on various currencies.

The FX industry is available every day, five days per week. There is no mystery. Indeed, global foreign exchange markets comprise loans, various business businesses, central banks, hedge funds, investment management companies, and retail Forex brokers, as well as global shareholders. The bulk of major global companies have several branches around the world on the Interbank Forex market so that they can transfer overseas swap instructions to their local customers at any moment during the 24 hours in an associated office.

Typically, this method is performed properly at any time of the week, unless bank holidays are disrupted. The banks operated at each national bureau during standard company hours, and the accessible trading catalog is generally transmitted to another national bureau in a subsequent time area.

During the Forex sessions, the session will be titled during the business hours of the city with the major financial hub in the relevant timezone. If you try to analyze the best time to trade currency pairs, it is essential to know what currencies or prices in those business hours and what Forex meetings are most liquid.

As this industry works in various time zones, it is available almost at any time of the day. Also, the international currency industry is not dominated by a single market, but rather by a worldwide network of markets and brokers. Trading hours in each involved nation are focused on when trading is available.

Major sessions are:

- London session
- US session
- London/US Overlap
- Tokyo session

Minor sessions are:

- Wellington/Auckland
- Sydney
- Frankfurt
- Hong Kong
- Singapore

As one significant FX industry ends, another industry starts. The trend continues to follow. Sometimes, and it is essential to maintain a record of them, they are more involved. For example, New York is 8 am to 5 pm ETE, Tokyo from 7 pm to 4 pm EST, Sydney from 8 am to 2 pm EST, London from 3 pm to 12 pm EST. Sometimes the largest quantity of trades takes a position when economies intersect.

Using the Demo Account

Traders with a demo account are also able to trade with a demo trading account without risk. That implies that traders can not jeopardize their assets and choose to relocate to private economies. The demo trading account of Admiral Markets allows a trader to have links to the recent information on the real-time industry, to trade in simulated currencies, and to specialist traders ' recent business ideas.

Trading sessions

One of the most important features of the overseas currency industry, as earlier described, is that it is available 24 hours a day. Investors worldwide can do company during ordinary company hours, after a job and even during the evening. However, not every time is produced entirely equivalent. There are worldwide forex trading moments when price action is steadily fluctuating, and periods also exist when it is totally silent.

Due to the overall demographics of those business respondents who are shopping in that specific moment, multiple currency pairs show distinct behavior over various moments of the trading day. This leads us to recognize that significant Forex trading meetings are immediately linked to market time.

Although a 24-hour industry provides many personal and corporate traders with a significant benefit as it ensures liquidity and a strong chance to trade within fixed Forex trade hours at any moment, it does not lack some flaws. While different currencies can be traded whenever you want, for such long periods, a trader can not track a situation.

That means that Forex trading periods will be available when there are missed chances, or even worse, where price volatility jumps lead to a set position being rejected if the trader is not close by. A trader must be conscious of the most frequently volatile industry, thus identify what moments are appropriate for the personal trading strategy and trade type, in an attempt to decrease that danger.

The industry is usually divided into three business meetings at its pinnacle: Asian, European, and North American. More frequently, Forex is also called the Tokyo, London, and New York meetings for these three trading hours.

The designations of these three towns are used interchangeably simply as they constitute the main economic centers for each region. When those three power companies operate-because, most companies and companies conduct regular operations-the economies are most involved. An increased density of speculators is also available internet.

Asia Trading Sessions

When liquidity returns to the Forex market after weekends, it is natural that Asian markets are the first to take an intervention. Asian trading meetings or Tokyo sessions This is the beginning of Forex market trading hours. The Tokyo investment exchanges are depicted by activities (although not formally) from this portion of the globe, which reside between 00:00 and 06:00 GMT. Nonetheless, many others, including Australia, China, NZ, and Russia, have significant pulls during this era.

Given the scattering of such economies, it allows sense for the Asian meeting to begin and finish beyond Forex's standard time in Tokyo. In reality, Asian hours are often regarded to be between 23:00-08:00 GMT to allow for the operations of these distinct industries.

European Trading Session

Later in the trading day, just before the end of Asian hours of trading, a European session will continue to keep currency markets active. European trading session or London session This Forex time zone for trading is very thick, covering a range of important financial markets. London is honored to identify the European meeting parameters.

London's Official hours of a company operate from 07:30 to 15:30 GMT. Due to other capital markets, including Germany and France, this trading duration is extended before formal opening in the United Kingdom, while volatility is repressed as long as London is closed after the trading meeting. Consequently, the European Forex GMT trading time between 07:00–16:00 GMT is generally noted.

North American Trading Session

The Asian markets were already closed for a couple of hours as North America's trading session or New York session. But for the traders in the European FX, the day is halfway through. The Western part-session is affected by exercise in the United States, with some additions from Canada, Mexico, and other South American nations. Not amazingly, New York activities are highly volatile, as well as attendance at the meeting on the GMT business hours of North American Forex.

Given premature business operation in the financial markets, stock trading, and noticeable accumulation of economic launches, the official beginning of North American hours at 12:00 GMT is unofficial. The liquidity interval is established at the conclusion of New York's trading at 20:00 GMT with a considerable break between the closing of US banks and the closing hours of the Asian Forex market, as the North American meeting ends.

Forex Hours And Meetings Overlaps

The European / Asian meeting will result in a much larger reaction of monetary pairs that are most active during European and Asian Forex hours (such as GBP / JPY and EUR / JPY) and thus a reduced rise in cost intervention during the EU-North American meeting. Nevertheless, irrespective of whether the couple or the components ' corresponding meetings have a substantive impact on the operation of each currency.

Asian / European overlapping is shown in pairs traded strongly over Asian and European forex hours. During pair effective business hours, long-term or basic FX traders who try to find a place could contribute to a low admission cost, missed access, or trading that is contrary to the strategy. On the other side, volatility is certainly crucial for short-term traders who have no place tonight or even forever.

Non-Trading Risky Business Hours

There is significant trade danger during poor liquidity, generally when a stock starts and around 12 AM. In the ordinary course of trading hours, lower liquidity could result in higher volatility. The trade traders do not suggest anywhere between 12-2 AM starting locations. Most of these high threat moments might jeopardize a trader's account.

Risk variables include:

A volatility spike–Low liquidity can quickly trigger volatility peaks to your halt lose or slow

Liquidity–This has to do with the size of the forex market and has to do with the capacity to manage big operations efficiently —

Dealing spreads: spreads typically extend at approximately 12 am.

The Best Time To Trade Market

Traders then strive to discover the finest trading options. The TOTH (Top Of The Hour) will generally provide volatility and spicy stock activities the first and last five hours of each hour.

In Forex, a market participant must first determine whether their personal trading approach works finest with elevated or low volatile volatility. If price action is more essential, it could be preferable to exchange business, overlap with the meeting, or just normal financial moments. The next stage is to decide on the finest Forex trading hours or moments, considering the volatility preference. Those who wish to be highly volatile must define the most effective timeframe for the currency pair to be traded on.

The European / North America Crossover Session will discover the most motion when assessing the EUR / USD couple. There are generally options, and an FX dealer should combine physical well-being with the need for good business circumstances. For example, if a US market participant prefers to trade the active Forex open hours, for GBP / JPY, it needs to wake up very early in the morning to stay on the market.

This could result in significant exhaustion and errors in judgment when trading if this individual also has periodic work. The European / North American border, which still has elevated volatility, could provide a much larger option for this trader.

Moreover, a good agreement of knowledge of how the Forex finest trading hours can provide a benefit in aspects of trade currencies, combined with an overall understanding of FX Trading Sessions.

CHOOSING A BROKER AND AVOIDING FOREX TRADING FRAUD

Opening a foreign trading card is a job that needs steel nerves, particularly for those who do not know the scheme. You could have learned of many Forex opponents who made people lose their hard-earned cash all because they fall victim to ineffective and false brokers. Such fraudsters typically enroll their business as unique formal foreign exchange brokers. It encourages prospective customers to access their records and ultimately mix up the stored money.

With such brokers, entry to hard-earned money is not unusual. After a customer seeks the removal of money, the provider continues to fulfill the application after opening the register. The fraudsters completely disregard the application or discover different grounds for withholding the money. You just near the file sometimes. This generally occurs with people not living in the nation or region where the broker is enrolled. Otherwise, you would be able to charge them and lodge a fraud request.

Most of us will want to select a stockbroker at some stage. Both stockbrokers and most utility companies differ widely. The selection of a broker is about priority and what you appreciate. Maybe your first selection for a courier does not have all you want, but be confident it has the main stuff.

Choosing A Brokerage Service?

If you really need to invest, you must have a brokerage company account. Here we find what a brokerage is and the types of brokerage companies. We also recognize considerations when selecting a brokerage or how to start an office once a choice has been taken.

What Is A Brokerage?

A brokerage is a company that allows trading of financial securities between customers and vendors, like stocks, mutual funds, and bonds. As an investor, you can purchase and exchange securities with a brokerage account.

Brokerages create cash by paying both customers, vendors, and other management fees, such as card maintenance fees, each moment they perform business. A few kinds of brokerages, including complete duty brokers, discount brokers, and Robo-consultants, are available.

What is a complete service broker?

A full-service broker provides thorough economic guidance, scheduling, and implementation to its clients, including choosing and managing an investment. Some full-time brokers also have instructions and facilities for pension, property or income schedules. They generally provide a broad range of investment and provide their clients with internal inventory research and assessment. The agents generally provide the costly choice as they provide services and services on behalf of their clients to pay high Commissions, consultative fees and maintenance fees for each customer.

As many complete business brokers gain cash from each item they offer, a dispute of concern can be created that some brokers advise equity products not appropriate for an investor. Some full-service brokers pay only advice or fixed charges to eliminate this dispute of concern and can reduce the general customer fee.

What Is A Discount/Online Broker?

Discount / Online Brokers are ideal for buyers who want to do it themselves. They do not provide investment advice, but some studies and evaluations of business can be carried out without cost. It is the investment and the performance of a business by investors using a discount / online dealer. Investors

Since discount brokers don't give all the whistles and keys of a complete duty dealer, it is much less expensive to use. You don't pay consultative charges, and your transaction commissions are generally significantly smaller than a complete business agent. Furthermore, many do not pay repair charges for the account.

The Term Robo Advisor?

The middle ground among complete business agents and discount / online brokers is occupied by robotic consultants. An internet financial advisor is a Robo consultant who develops an integrated investment portfolio for his clients, yet who does not provide a natural consultant. Like full-service brokers, Robo consultants choose investors and perform business on behalf of clients. As there is no natural contact, they are not able to fully customize a fund, manage specific equity requirements or provide guidance on other matters such as pension provision or taxation. Instead of paying an advice premium, which is generally much smaller than the complete duty courier, many Robo advisors pay no license payment.

Things To Take Account Of When Selecting A Brokerage

Where to spend your cash with so many brokerage services on the sector can be hard to make. Investors must take into account a multitude of cost-to-trade variables during the assessment of a dealer.

Do you need a Discount Broker or Full-Service Broker?

It may be incredible to jump into a premium courier first and select your shares yourself if you are fresh to investment. If you want guidance on your assets, a full-service broker or Robo consultant can create meaning. Full utility brokers can also be perfect for people with complex equity requirements or economic circumstances. Robo consultants are a happy middle ground for the investor, who doesn't want to receive full-service courier charges, but who still seeks a more disadvantageous investment strategy. If you wish to do something about yourself, then the easiest and cheapest alternative is probably a discount / online dealer.

What Are Charges And Fees?

You should check their fees and charges timeline before entering an office with a brokerage company to know how and when your charges come. Fees and other expenses can erode your yields rapidly and even consume your main resources. Some couriers may have a concealed fee that is difficult to determine— in this situation. You should email customer service to reply to all your inquiries about the charges. You can easily assess the annual fee for each dealer to create distinction if you understand how much you will invest, and how often you will buy or sell it.

What Are Minimum Accounts?

Some brokerage services involve very large accounts to access an office (particularly complete business brokers). Some may involve their clients to keep a minimum amount on their account in order to prevent extra charges. If you're fresh to spend or have little to spend, then entering a brokerage account may be an obstacle. However, do not despair— many brokers do not have minimum demands for closing or balancing.

What Kind Of Account Will You Open And What Are You Investing In?

The range of services offered by most dealers includes pension, taxable, and custodial records. Additional charges or charges may be connected, depending on the sort of account you wish to access. For instance, IRAs usually have closure or transaction charges greater than those for a periodic brokerage account.

Investors in conventional stocks, bonds, and other resources, but not all brokerages, are permitted to spend in more complicated and riskier securities such as centigrade stocks, foreign currencies, or alternatives. You should look for a brokerage that provides these assets to an affordable price if you wish to invest in this type of securities.

How Often Do You Trade?

If you intend to trade openly, perform various businesses weekly or daily, a brokerage that provides small transaction fees should be considered. Trading charges and commissions are less important for buy-and-hold companies (companies that rarely trade).

Does Any Commission Brokerage Offer Free Products Or Sign-Up Bonuses?

Two of the most common products some brokers give are free swap traded bonds (ETFs) and shared savings without transaction fees. To protect your yields on your investment, spending cash on commissions and duties is essential when you plan to spend in mutual funds and ETFs in your inventory primarily. Some couriers even operate their own mutual funds and ETFs, in which their clients can participate without paying charges. Also, the fresh office openers are frequently encouraged by internet brokerages. Cash bonuses and free trades-test our brokerage offers and bonus manual. These registration benefits can assist you in reducing the total transaction costs.

Is The Brokerage Offering Investment Research Or Other Benefits?

Investment study, like an assessment of particular assets or market trends, is a significant tool for many shareholders, and, if not free, the performance and cost vary widely between brokers. Other facilities, like internet control, debit Card facilities, or portfolio diversification facilities, are also provided by some brokerage companies. Many of those rewards and benefits provided, however, have stringent criteria which can include original payment or withdrawal limitations. Before you sign up, scan the good text to guarantee that you are qualified for the bid and know what it means.

What Is The Experience Of Our Customers?

Simply speaking, some brokerage systems are more user-friendly and superior to other brokers ' services. Some clients do not carry out business with a minimal cost if it is more difficult to operate the Website or if the customer service is only accessible at certain hours. An excellent client knowledge could create a large distinction in purchasing knowledge for shareholders who are not technologically knowledgeable.

Even though you are tech-savvy, it's nice to understand that if you have any issues with your application, you can contact a client service agent, text, or text. A lot of discounts/ online brokers are only present internet. While this can assist in cutting expenses, general customer service can also be affected. Some brokers also pay heavy broker support charges. If you believe that you may need broker support for your business, imagine choosing a broker with the existence of brick and mortar.

Opening A Brokerage Account

Once you click on a brokerage, you will want to start afresh account with them. They will need you to log in to your brokerage card data and take several choices. Some of the data a brokerage will ask you may contain: —

Basic private information, such as title, address and e-mail address, place of birth—·

Social security Number (needed by national agencies)

The government of the country provided IDs, including the driver's permit or passport.

- ✓ Employment status
- ✓ Annual income and net worth
- ✓ Type of account
- ✓ Investment objectives

The normal brokerage account is a cash account, and that is what fresh shareholders should select. You can purchase cash from the brokerage to spend on a premium fund, and earn tax on the cash you have lent. Margin reports involve a range of hazards and typically are not suggested for the median investor.

You will be told to finance the plan when you have finished the documents for the application. Most brokers allow you to finance your business from a check or loan card. In some circumstances, a wire transfer or a check may also be completed. It might bring several days before your deposit shows the resources. You can start buying once the money is accessible in your portfolio.

RISK MANAGEMENT (FOREX)

Risk management is one of the most commonly discussed topics in commerce. Traders wish, on the one hand, to reduce the potential waste, but, on the other hand, these traders are interested in taking full advantage of one trade. It's no secret that you need to put more risks in order to get the best returns.

This is the question of appropriate risk management. The present document addresses the risk management for forex trading and the governance of the forex threat during trading. This can help prevent risks and contribute without worry about your company.

What Is The Risk Of Forex?

The Forex market is one of the world's biggest financial markets, with revenues totaling more than US$ 1.4 trillion a day. There is thus the opportunity for enormous profit and loses for banks, economic institutions, and personal shareholders. Forex trading risk is merely the possible loss or benefit resulting from changes in swap prices. Each investor must have some risk management measures, strategies and precautions in Forex to minimize the probability of financial loss.

Many individuals are involved in foreign-exchange trading operations today. But most of them are not able to make the earnings they hope. Some traders lose all the money. Some don't get their anticipated outcomes. Actually, only a tiny part of traders can fulfill their requirements or even exceed them. The forex market is evolving continually, and all traders have to operate with excellent hazards. The Forex trade risk management topic is, therefore, becoming increasingly common among Forex traders.

Forex is the trading of currency pairs or foreign exchange. For example, if you go long on EUR / USD, you hope that the value of the Euro in comparison to the United States will increase. Dollar. Dollar. You could think mistaken, as with any venture, and the trade could go against you. This is the clearest danger for the FX market trading. You can take extra danger by trading in less popular currency pairs (and thus less liquid) and by becoming volatile as the transaction itself does not manage your margin account correctly, or you chose an ineffective broker or trading exchange!

It is worth remembering that the vast bulk of forex operations are done by companies rather than by people, and effectively use forex to decrease the danger of fluctuations in currencies. In your computerized business systems, you use complicated algorithms to handle some of the following hazards. As a person, many of these hazards are less present, and others can be minimized via proper business management. Any enterprise that provides potentially profitable income also has an adverse danger to the extent that it loses much more than the price of the equity transfer. This chapter can assist you to know the hazards to succeed with trade.

The following are the major risk factors in FX trading:

- ✓ Exchange Rate Risk
- ✓ Interest Rate Risk
- ✓ Credit Risk

- ✓ Country Risk
- ✓ Liquidity Risk
- ✓ Marginal or Leverage Risk
- ✓ Transactional Risk
- ✓ Risk of Ruin

Exchange Rate Risk

The risk of the exchange rate is the uncertainty of currency price modifications. It is focused on the impact on the global supply and requests the equilibrium of constant and generally fluid changes. The location of the trader shall be excluded for the duration during which it shifts prices. This danger can be very significant and is focused on the perception of the market of how the currencies can progress depending on all feasible variables that happen (or can take place) wherever around the globe. Moreover, because Forex off-exchange trade is mainly unregulated, a controlled futures exchange does not impose any weekly price limit. The industry passes based on basic and technical variables–more on subsequently.

The most common method of trade is to cut costs and drive lucrative roles to ensure that profits are maintained within manageable boundaries. This method of common sense includes: the threshold of a situation

Position limit

A position is the maximal quantity of currency which is permitted to be carried at any moment by a trader.

Loss limit

The loss threshold is a metric that aims to prevent unsustainable transfers by traders by establishing halt loss rates. You need to avoid ordering losses. It is essential.

Simple Risk / Rewards Rates

An easy approach is used by traders to evaluate their desired profits against probable failures as a guideline when attempting to regulate exchange rate risk. The concept is to lose the majority of traders as long as they profit, so keeping your risk/reward percentage to 1:3 is an easy approach to trading.

Interest Rate Risk

Interest rating threat relates to earnings and losses produced by changes in forwarding yields, mismatch in future amounts, and settlement differences in foreign currency operations. This danger is relevant for currency exchanges, forward, future and choices. One lays the boundaries on the complete magnitude of mismatches to minimize the danger of interest rates. One way of working together is to divide the mismatches into up to six months and six months, depending on their age levels. In an attempt to calculate locations for every shipping date, gain, and loss, all operations are registered in computer processes. To predict any adjustments that may affect exceptional differences, a continuous assessment of the interest rate setting is essential.

Credit Risk

Credit threat relates to the likelihood, because of a counterparty's compulsory or unlawful intervention, of not repaying an outstanding monetary stance as decided. Credit risk is generally a problem of businesses and companies. The credit risk for personal traders (equity trading) is very small, as this also applies to enterprises enrolled in G-7 nations and controlled under them. The NFA and the Commodity Futures Trading Commission (CFTC) have established their authority over the US FX exchanges in the latest years and proceed to oppose unregistered FX companies. Western European countries adopt the Financial Services Authority's rules in Great Britain. This agency has the strictest laws in each nation to ensure that FX businesses are safe in their jurisdiction. All traders need to verify businesses carefully before transferring any trading money.

Most businesses are pleased to reply to customer requests and frequently publish on their internet notices concerning the safety of assets. Nevertheless, it must be noted that the minimum capital requirements for Futures Commission Merchants (FCMs) recorded with the CFTC, which are much lower than those of the banks, does not extend to funds deposited for collateralization in off-exchange currency trading under the current CFTC regulations and NFA rules protective provisions concerning the separation of customer funds in the regulated future accounts. For these and other factors, the CFTC and NFA reject any depiction that Futures Commission Merchant's registry position significantly decreases Forex over-the-counter trading hazards.

The known forms of credit risk are:

Replacement risk

Replacement risk happens when a bank or Forex broker's counterparties are aware that they are in danger of not getting their money from the unsuccessful bank.

Settlement risk

The danger of settlement is due to time zones that differ on distinct islands. Settlement risk, As a result, currencies may be traded on various trading days at separate rates. Australian and New Zealand Dollars are first credited to the country, followed by the Japanese Yen, the European currency and the US dollar. Payment may, therefore, be produced previous to the execution of the own transactions by a group that declares insolvency or is proclaimed insolvent.

When evaluating credit risk, the trader must take account not only of its monetary portfolio's market value but also of its future exposures.

A probability assessment can be used to determine the prospective spread through the moment of mature of the situation. In the application of credit risk strategies, computerized systems presently accessible are helpful. It's easy to monitor credit rows. Furthermore, traders use corresponding schemes in foreign exchange, which were implemented since April 1993, to carry out credit policy. Traders enter for a particular counterparty the complete lines of loan. The credit line is automatically adapted during the trade meeting. The scheme prevents the trader from interacting further with that counterparty when it is fully used. The credit line will return to its initial rate after mature.

Counterparties default risk

The place and forward contracts of Over-the-Counter (OTC) are not trade in currency; instead, funds and FCM are typically responsible for the operation of the exchange. Given that the execution of place and forward-looking agreements on currencies is not guaranteed by swap or saving houses of currency, the customer is exposed to counter-party risks–the danger of being unable or refused by the managers with a traders, the trader group, or the FCM or their counterparties with whom the company or FCM trade. Moreover, local and prospective managers are not obliged to keep trading spot markets and forward agreements.

Furthermore, the non-centralized aspect of the exchange sector can cause the complications mentioned above: A bank or FCM may neglect to carry out an offer in a currency market that it thinks is more risky than appropriate to its activities. Since no main filing system is in place to ensure OTC trade, each company or FCM must use its threat assessment to decide whether to engage in a specific industry, where its lending must be behind every trade. A particular bank or FCM may refuse to fulfill an offer made by a trader/customer depending on the policy of any counterparty. It has sometimes occurred and will certainly occur once again in reaction to volatile business circumstances.

Since the core bank does not distribute minute-by-minute and advertising accounts, companies and the FCMs need to depend on their own understanding and acceptance of the implementation cost of current stock exchange rates. In large part, the execution price for a trader/customer reflects the bank or FCM's know-how in the trading of the given currency. Although the OTC interbank industry, in its entirety, is extremely fluid, some currencies, recognized as exotics, are traded by some but the biggest retailers less often. For that purpose, a less skilled counterpart may leave time to complete an offer or may be awarded a performance cost, which varies considerably from that of a more seasoned or greater counterpart. As a result, in moments of elevated business volatility, the exchange levels of two members trading on the same exchanges through various counterparties may differ significantly.

The counterparties' economic collapse could lead to significant casualties. Again, the merchant/customer is responsible to organizations since police officers and organizations, when trading foreign currencies for reasons of OTC, can be prone to failure or insolvency. For such bankruptcies or losses, the trader can only recover, concerning property that is specifically traceable to his account, the proportional share of all of the properties available to distribute to all of its customers.

If the trader and customer property recorded with an FCM is covered with the limited regulation safety given for in the customer's segregation laws and procedures, customer goods transmitted to OTC Foreign Exchange trading secure or compensated for are not safeguarded, as the FCMs shall be disqualified from national legislation under the Customer Trading Center (FCM).

Country And Liquidity Risk

While the liquidity of OTC Forex is generally significantly greater than the futures in currencies traded on the exchange, there were nonetheless periods of illiquidity, particularly outside the US and European trade hours. Moreover, in the previous several countries or organizations of countries have placed trade boundaries or limitations on the quantity by which, over a moment, the prices of some foreign currency prices may differ or have constraints or penalties enforced in respect of the holding of posts in certain foreign currencies during certain periods or volumes traded. Such restrictions may discourage the execution of trades during a particular trade era. Such constraints or limitations may stop a trader from immediately liquidating unfavorable stocks and thus could cause significant damages to the trader's account. In other cases, the General Partner may not be able to execute the trade at favorable prices even though the price of foreign exchange does not fall within government restrictions if the liquidity of the market is insufficient. The country or the band of nations can also limit currency movement across national boundaries; stop or limit trade or trade-in certain currencies; issue entirely different currencies in an attempt to replace ancient currencies; order the immediate resolution of certain monetary debt, or command only for liquidation to be ordered in a certain monetary. OTC Forex is traded on a range of non-US exchanges, which may be owing to several variables be significantly more likely to occur during phases of non-liquidity than the US.

Furthermore, even if halt losses or limited orders are placed to try and restrict profits, these commands may not be executed on very illiquid economies or may be executed at unforeseeable prices when the execution is not more favorable, even when there are no liquidity or excessive volatility instructions.

Leverage Risk

In the foreign exchange (as for controlled product options), low-margin payments or trading bonds are usually needed. These marginal strategies allow a strong advantage. Therefore, comparatively tiny cost motion can lead to instant and significant damages exceeding the quantity spent in the agreement. For example, if 10 percent of the contract price was placed based on the margins at the time of purchase, the total loss of margin before the brokerage commission deduction would result in a 10 percent decrease in the contract price if the contract was concluded after that. The complete failure of the premium payment would lead to a reduction of more than 10 percent. Certain traders may choose to deposit up to 100% of their

Foreign Exchange trading account resources. Händlers should know that the violent use of leverage increases casualties during unfavorable results phases.

Transactional Risk

In the case of interaction, processing, and verification of commands of a trader, errors can cause unforeseen casualties (sometimes referred to as "out-trades"). Even if an outsourcing trade is largely due to the counterparty negotiating body, it can be restricted in pursuing payment for corresponding damages in the fund to the trader/customer's remedy.

Risk Of Ruin

Even if the medium-to-long-term view of the market in a trader/customer is finally correct, the trader may not be financially responsible for short-term, unrealized losses and may close a position to a loss simply because they can not fulfill or otherwise hold a margin call. Thus traders with a lack of assets may face loss, even if the trader's opinion of the industry is right and a monetary stance may eventually be reversing and profiting if kept.

Stay back from possibilities that seem too great to be real. Generally, speeding up systems is usually a fraud. For instance, prevent a forex business that predicts or ensures high profitability. If a business claims in one month that it is going to double or maximize your cash or guarantees a monthly yield, wander back. Stay back from forex businesses promising little financial risk or no danger. Trading forex is certainly risky; if anyone says the opposite to you, they are not true. Keep in mind that forex companies make the following kind of statements: "Whatever the market is moving, you can not lose" or "With a risk, it's largely outweighed by the reward." If you can't fulfill yourself that people are lawful and overshadowed, the best way is to prevent trading in them.

FOREX TRADING PSYCHOLOGY

Forex trading psychology is a great thing. Often it is the psychology that is seen as the main cause of commercial errors and not an absence of academic knowledge or skill in implementation. Financial traders from different domestic, cultural, and social backgrounds continually repeat errors, suggesting that these errors are based on the common features shared among us as human beings.

This prevalent feature is fear, which produces the human reaction of "battle or flight." This fight or flight reaction, unfortunately, can cause a large number of traders to collapse. We can't alter what we have experienced over millions of years; however, by looking into the psychology of successful forex traders and then implementing the results, we can alter how we approach those emotions. We will today examine how we deal with the right Forex trading psychology and react to trade conditions.

The impact on trading behavior can be considerably limited by fear. Naturally, the safest way to guarantee survival will be found in your thoughts. When it comes to trade, this implies that you have a natural instinct to get out of the trade if a trade looks like it will lose profit, so you will not be incurring any further losses.

This can, however, help you avoid a thoroughly scheduled trading strategy. Even worse, you can make rash choices in the hope that the trade will be lost and you will lose much more cash than you would have had to leave it. You want to concentrate on making the most of that brief losing situation instead of focussing on the long-term strategy.

Understanding the role of forecast psychology will help you alleviate your concern about your decision making. Know the fear both as a trader and as an individual on the site. It will also allow you to restore control of the logic and reason that is your ultimate goal.

Type Of Trading Bias

It's simple for traders to feel confident that during trade meetings, they can stay calm and gathered before market access is open. It is a distinct story; however, once the clock begins. It is very simple for feelings to come into play in the face of actual economic choices. But we can learn to work around them. We can not prevent our feelings.

Traders can't allow themselves to be excited, scared, or covetous when they trade because it can cause expensive and irreversible errors. Psychologically evaluate yourself by finding out that you face a psychological prejudice of Forex Trading: the overconfidence prejudice:' The market will go here' / the anchoring preference;" This means, likely,' / or confirmation-' this also demonstrates that I'm right.'-" I hope the price comes back. However, it is the first important step to become conscious of our feelings that we will discuss in detail.

Over-Confidence Bias

In Forex trading psychology, over-confidence Bias is to watch for euphoria. Naturally, people are self-oriented. Our egos want to be validated by demonstrating that we are better than the average person and understand what we do. Any indication that confirms these ideas only strengthens our own self-image through a separate sense of self-love.

The issue is that traders are likely to fall prey to over trust. It is not unusual for traders to make a winning streak and think that in the future, nothing can be incorrect. This is naturally unwise to think, and will only end in failure. Check your trading meetings and check your winnings and losses in detail.

Only then can you keep up with your trade? Let me make mistakes— and not make the mistake that I fear you will be in a much better condition during the long term. You have to recognize that mistakes are inevitable, especially in the early stages. It's all components of the learning curve.

Anchoring Bias

This is about the fields of mind comfort that traders develop during market analysis, believing that the future will eventually be the same as the present and only because the present feels like the past. It is borrowed from social research, as well as other requirements in forex psychology.

Anchoring tends to depend instead of looking at fresh circumstances and modifications that can take on something already known to the trader for decision-making in the future. Sometimes, anchoring causes traders to depend on data that is outdated and meaningless, which, of course, will not assist them to trade effectively.

This is demonstrated in practice by traders keeping losing positions overdue merely because they do not consider the alternatives outside the comfort zone. When trading Forex, you can not be scared to try fresh products-you are prepared to try fresh approaches and go against what you know. You can only increase your chances of losing more by anchoring you on obsolete policies and information.

Confirmation Bias

The one factor most prevalent among professional traders is confirmation bias. The search for data to support your choice, although it was not the best choice, is merely a way to justify your activities and policies. The issue is that you are not improving your techniques in reality by doing so, and you will only make the same trade errors. Sadly, this can generate an infinite loop that can be hard to break in forex trading psychology.

A trader merely spends valuable time searching for what he knows to be true is the best situation for a confirmatory biasing. The worst situation, however, is that it loses not only time but money and trade motivation. A trader must learn and use his intellect to create lucrative policies and then pursue them without fear or doubt.

The Aversion Bias For Loss

Aversion Loss comes from the hypothesis of prospects. Human beings have a funny way to assess their gains and losses and to compare their perceived meanings. For instance, we are prepared to give preference to a reduced loss than a greater possible reward in considering our alternatives before making a decision. Fear is a much stronger driver than covetousness. A dealer with a loss bias is, in reality, closer to reducing earnings when they are still small and allow for greater discounts.

There is one piece of guidance available to fix trader's issues that are derived from the study of Forex trading psychology–the development and adherence to a trading scheme. As a dubious trader, you should certainly be free to find every possible other solution, but you are likely to return to easy trading schemes. For traders, it's understandable to be afraid when they trade.

However, it is totally important for every trader who wishes to succeed to push this fear aside and do it. Trade, take notes, investigate, and create errors in fresh approaches. Testing and mistakes are a major component of the forex learning curve, and generations of traders have shown that this is the most efficient way of eliminating commercial concerns.

FOREX FUNDAMENTAL AND TECHNICAL ANALYSIS

Fundamental Analysis

Fundamental analysis is a technique for the assessment and the pricing of financial markets. The basic Forex assessment relies on the general economic status and investigates multiple variables such as interest rates, jobs, GDP, international trade, and production, as well as the comparative effect of this on the importance of the national currency in respect of which they connect.

In Forex, as well as in other financial markets, the basic assumption of fundamental analysis is that an asset's price may vary from its worth. Therefore, different economies can often misprice an asset, excess price, or short-term underprice. Fundamentalists say that, although the goods are priced at short notice, they will eventually back to the right value. The ultimate objective of fundamental analysis is to find an asset's true value, contrast it to present prices and identify a trading chance.

There is also clearly demonstrated the principal difference between fundamental and technical analysis. While the technical analysis does not pay much thought to anything other than the present cost, fundamental analysis studies all but the present cost. While it is possible that basic analytics may not be the finest instrument for a short term trader on daily exchanges, it is the basic variables of Forex and how they analyze the long-term response.

FX fundamental analysis methodology is not only about contrasting present information with prior figures for the final economic indicators. A wide range of economic theories revolves around basic forex assessment, trying to contextualize different parts of economic data and create them similarly.

The most common theory of monetary fundamentals is the concept of parity–a situation for the exchange of prices in line with local financial variables, such as unemployment and exchange levels, where currencies are adapted.

Good News-Bad News

You may have found that it's news accounts that generate movement in the economies from the most practical point of view of an ordinary Forex trader. How is that happening, and why? Financial specialists follow several economic indicators because they can give clues about the economy's safety.

These indices are presented in media accounts and news agencies. Some of them are published daily, most of them monthly and a couple of quarters. These messages and events can be tracked by the Forex Calendar. Now let us use the frequency of information releases to combine technical and fundamental analysis.

In the event of fundamental analyses of monetary trading, fresh information comes every second as a value citation, while basic statistics are released at most once a week. Capital is gradually flowing from nations in which the accumulation is possibly slowing relative with nations in which it could possibly grow at a quicker pace.

It's all about the power of an economy. If an economy is expected to be powerful, it will be an appealing location for foreign investment, as the return on financial markets will be greater.

After this, shareholders must first transfer their assets to the country's currency in issue in an attempt to spend. If you purchase more of that currency, supply will increase, and the currency will value it. Unfortunately, finance is not that easy, and that is why science does not know precisely instances of good markets that show declining currencies. Currencies do not reflect the status of the economy as an inventory of the business.

Currencies are also instruments that political decision-makers can manipulate, such as key institutions and even personal traders such as George Soros.

Traders and shareholders will search for indications of strengths or weaknesses in various markets when financial accounts are published. If consumer feeling moves in one manner before the news releases, value change before the publication is regarded as a' market cost.' The real information disclosure frequently creates some confusion.

In reverse, serious business volatility can happen if the industry is uncertain–or if the information findings differ from what was expected. For this reason, Forex rookie traders are usually recommended to remain back from the media when they perform basic assessments.

Major economic indicators Economic data may suggest changes in the financial position of a nation in question.

Interest rates

Interest levels are a key forex assessment measure. Interest levels There are many different types of interest prices, but we will concentrate here on nominal or basic main bank interest levels. Central banks generate cash, and then personal companies borrow cash. The level or rule by which personal companies reward central banks for lending currencies is referred to as the basis or nominal frequency. Whenever the sentence "interest prices" is heard, it is generally referred to by individuals.

One of the key banks ' main tasks is the manipulation of exchange prices-a large component of the domestic financial or fiscal strategy. The reason why interest rates are a major driver for the economy is that. Interest rates may be greater and impact monetary characteristics than any other variable. It can affect inflation, capital, trade, output, and joblessness

The key companies usually want to increase their economies and achieve an unemployment rate established by the government, thus lowering interest prices consequently. This stimulates both personal and personal lending as well as expenditure, manufacturing, and the economy as a whole. Low prices could be a nice approach, but a bad one.

In the long term, the low rates of interest can inflate the economy with cash and create economic bubbles that sooner or later, if not whole economies, will react to the collapse of the chain in the economy.

Central banks may also boost interest rates in order to prevent this, thereby reducing lending prices and giving companies, companies, and persons less cash to work with. The greatest location to begin looking for business possibilities from a Forex fundamental analysis viewpoint is the shifting interest rates.

Inflation

Inflation news releases about inflation reporting over time changes in the costs of products. Note that each economy has a "good growth" rate. The quantity of cash in storage, the meaning of unemployment, should increase over a long era as the country develops. The challenge is to stabilize regulators and central banks at this stage.

Too much inflation pushes supply-to-supply equilibrium, and the currency depreciates because it is just more than required. Deflation is the opposite hand of the currency card. The price of cash rises during deflation, while products and facilities are lower.

In the short term, it could be a good thing, but it can be a bad thing for the economy over the long term. Money is economic energy. Less energy is equivalent to less motion. Deflation may, at some stage, have a dramatic effect on a nation in that it is hard enough cash for the economy to continue, not to mention for the economy.

GDP

The GDP is the metric of all products and facilities generated by a nation within that era. GDP is thought to be the economy's highest general safety economic indicator. This may seem strange, particularly in the context of GDP, but it has no connection to the demand for these products and facilities. GDP measures the supply.

The general idea is that it is important to create rational, precise estimates both of production and demand. The belief that GDP represents both ends of the economy would not be wise. The rise in GDP, therefore, is the very reverse of a good economy without the associated rise in the supply for or accessibility of the gross domestic product, from a basic forex view.

The three primary economic indicators used in Forex fundamental analysis are interest rates, inflation, and GDP. Compared with other variables, such as retail sales, capital flow, trade balances, and bond rates, and many extra macroeconomic and geopolitical variables, they are incompatible with the financial effect they can create. In addition, not only are economic indicators evaluated over a moment, but some also correlate cross-disciplines with border crossings.

It is essential to realize that there is much financial information published that affects the Forex market significantly. You must know how to create a basic forex assessment, an integral aspect of your business strategy for the prediction of industry changes, whether you want to or not.

What Is Technical Analysis?

Technical Analysis

Technical analysis is an assessment of price motion on a Forex monetary couple or another business chart. We can believe in technological evaluation or "T.A." as a kind of structure, brief, which traders use to research and exploit a market price motion.

The main explanation of why traders are using T.A. Predictions is to be made depending on the cost motion of the previous.

Technical experts think that the stock motion or cost intervention on a cost chart reflects all present business factors. So, if we think that all variables of the market are reflected via price movements, we only need to analysis and trade the markets apart from price because we don't need much more.

Technical analysts search for trends in the diagram which appear to be repeated; they create the trade advantage. The logic behind it is that, since people guide most price flow, certain trends are repeated in the industry as people appear to be repeated in their feelings and business interactions.

Technical analysis also includes teaching to evaluate the composition of the industry, discover patterns, support levels, and strength levels and usually teach to' read' the fluctuations of a sector. Here there is some choice, and I'm the first individual to say T.A. It's a science more than craft. That said, it's something that will comfort you and improve you at a certain point of moment and exercise. A.T. Shape the backbone of my key-value trading technique, which merely derives from or offshoots ' traditional T.A.' with more simplicity and more concise methods that do not include misleading forex indices or stuff such as Elliot Wave theory that is much too complicated and free to understanding to think that they are worth trading and learning.

The majority of traders believe of a cost graph as above when someone says' technical assessment' immediately Price charts give us an amazing amount of useful data, which gives an overview of the historical and current situation of the market and supply and demand as well as of the prices that are considered most important by market participants. Much of my price action trading class is based around studying how to define, and trades cost actions at the main level in the industry. We have to give unique consideration to these price standards because prices are generally respected over and over again. Also, prices reflect the views of all business respondents regarding the industry and business factors, so you can streamline your trade and simultaneously evaluate the end outcome of everything that adds to a stock motion of a sector by concentrating your assessment and trading on a value graph.

How To Make A Forex Trading Plan

One of the main factors to becoming a good Forex Trader is a forex trading strategy. Many traders never create a trading scheme, let alone frequently use it. You must make a plan of trade and make use of the one... do not just make one and never see it as many dealers do. You both need to do so.

Here are a couple of significant items that you have to remember in terms of Forex Trading plans.

- ✓ You must follow the scheme, have a newspaper and logging trade.
- ✓ Create a Forex trading strategy;
- ✓ develop (or use a current) Forex Trading Journal;
- ✓ ACTUALLY, use the Forex Trading Journal.

The method of developing a Forex Trading Plan for a good trading approach, such as price action trading, will strengthen your knowledge of the trading strategy and also give you an overview of what you need to do whenever you communicate. This business blueprint is crucial to the development of the sort of ice-cold practice needed to achieve long-term success in the Forex monetary sector.

Logging your trade-in a trading journal is crucial for your achievement, as it provides you with a graphic image of your capacity (or absence thereof) to trade on the exchanges, and it also generates a document that you can use that will demonstrate you how your trading edges play out in a moment.

A checklist that you pursue is to be included in your trade scheme, including what you are looking for in the industry and what you want to see before you start a trade. If you can tick all of the cabinets, you join your trade, unless you stop until the top of your business is restored. In reality, you can create your entire business plan as a checklist, making it a fluid structure, which enables you to decide rapidly if any prospective trading arrangements are worth following.

The primary reason to develop a Forex Trading Plan is that planning your business beforehand and determining what you are looking for on the exchanges are the best way to benefit from the long-term — trading plans and expectations. One important reason is because If you're not in the industry, you will never be calmer and more meaningful, so if you can schedule all the businesses you're not on, then when you are in a trade you are completely uninfluenced by business factors, and it works to safeguard you from an unexpected forex trader.

Patience and wait for the conditions of a plan to be developed– don't push the problem Patience may be the biggest attribute a forex trader can hold. It implies that when you're a careful trader, you're aware of what you need on the exchanges and wait until your trading border appears before you trade. Trading in this way eliminates many negative trades resulting from emotional... or patience-free trade. Much of the business, and possibly the biggest portion, is simply looking for an' optimal' pricing or other configuration to take place on the exchange. Traders who do not plan for an optimal set-up to shape, wind up wasting cash fast because they deny their market advantage. Make careful that you emphasize the significance of consistency in your trade scheme, every moment you write it. You will always recall how essential it is to be a careful trader to make cash for your Forex market.

FOREX ORDER TYPES

When you begin to understand the foundation of Forex Trading, you need to understand the order. Traders are using forex orders for trading in and out of the market during daytime trading and helping to regulate trading. There are many sorts. In certain contracts, traders can enter the market when prices are at a specific level, while in other orders, traders can enter or leave the market at the current price.

The word forex order merely relates to how you enter or exit an enterprise — type of forex orders. You can use a lot more alternatives, both now and in the future, if you trade for forex than buy and sell at the current market price, and we're going through your choices here.

It is highly essential that you understand how to place orders properly when placing orders with a forex broker. Orders should be put while you go business— that is how you plan to go into the market. Failure to place orders can skew your entry and exit points. Some of the most popular kinds of forex orders are discussed in this section.

This is the most prevalent form of order.

Market Order

Types You have the Bidder on the screen at this speed if you want to place an order immediately at the market cost. There is to be a market order. You can enter (purchase or sell) a new spot or exit the current situation with the market order (purchase or sell).

Stop Order

An order is given only when the price reaches. Order Stop You can join the present condition or leave it. A stop order must be ordered at a market price for a currency pair where your specified cost is higher than or equal to the premises on the market; the purchase price needs to be greater than the existing market price. A sales stop order is a specification for exchange rate sales of a currency pair if the price is or is less; the cost of these sales shall be less than the price current.

1. Stop orders are common when trading break-ups for entering a market. For example: assume USD / CHF rallies to a resistance level, and you think, based on your analysis, that it will continue to increase if it goes above the resistance level. To trade this opinion, you can order a couple of pipes higher than the resistance level so you can trade the upside-down potential. This will open up your long location if the price reaches or exceeds your specified price.

If you want to trade an outage of your downside, an entry stop order may also be used. Place a stop-sell order a few pipes below the support level to open your short position when the price reaches or goes below the specified price.

2.Consignments stop to limit your losses. Everyone has losses every now and then, but the biggest part is the size and manner in which you manage losses. You should have already an insight into where you wish to get out of position if the market turns against it before you even enter a trade. A predetermined stop order often referred to as a stop-loss, is one of the effective ways to limit losses.

Say, USD / CHF, if you have a long place, you want the pair to increase value. To avoid challenging unchecked losses, a stop-sell order can be placed at a certain price so that when this price is reached, your position is automatically closed.

A short position will have a stop-buy order instead.

1. Stop orders for profit protection may be used. Once your trade is lucrative, you can change your stop-loss order to safeguard some of your profit. If your business doesn't attain your defined profit-oriented goal and market changes against your trade, you can shift your stop-sell order to a lucrative area for a long time to protect against the possibility of a loss. Similarly, you can transfer your stop-buy order from loss to the profit area to safeguard your income in a short time it has become very lucrative.

Limit Order

If you are only prepared to join a fresh position or leave a position at or better certain prices, a limited order is put. The order shall be filled out only if the industry trades at or better that cost. An order for a limit-buy is instructions for you to purchase the currency pair at the market price once the rate you specify or is below the price you specify. A sale limit command is a command to sell the currency pair at the market price when your defined price or higher hits the market; that price must be greater than that of your present market price.

1. When you are a breakout, limited orders are usually used to enter a market. If you do not expect the currency value to break

through a successful resistance or support level, you will lose out. In other words, you expect the currency cost to rebuild the resistance to decrease or to increase its assistance.

For instance: presume you believe the present rally movement of USD / CHF will not effectively break the opposition based on your market assessment. So, if USD / CHF rallies up close to that opposition, it would be a great chance to shorten this. In order to benefit from this hypothesis, you can place a few pips below that resistance point in a limit order that fills your brief order if the market reaches this cost or greater.

In addition to using the limit order, this command can also be used to reach a support level for a long while. You may want to take this chance to go a long time, for example, to think of a high likelihood that the present decrease of USD / CHF is going to pause and reverse at some stage of assistance. In such cases, you can place a limit purchase order a couple of pipes above that support level in order to fill your long order as the market moves down to the specified price or below.

2. To set your profit target, limit orders are used. You should already have a concept, before you place your business, of where you want to profit if the trade goes your way. You can exit the industry by a limit order with your pre-fixed profit target. You will use this limit order to set your profit goal if you have been using a monetary couple. If you do not do so, the order for limit purchases should be used to set your profit target. Note that only rentable prices are accepted in those orders.

Run The Right Order

You will be able to use the appropriate tools to achieve your intentions–how you want to enter the market (trade or selling), and how you will quit the market (profit and loss). While other kinds of orders may exist— the most frequent are market, stop, and restrict orders. You can use them conveniently because incorrect order execution could cost you cash.

Forex orders play an essential part in the day-to-day business, and so it is essential to know the complications of the various kinds of trade orders for beginners. These are only the most prevalent. Many other orders can or cannot be provided, but if you can comprehend how each of these five works, you will be able to comprehend better how complex trading orders function.

TIPS FOR CHOOSING RELIABLE FOREX TRADE BROKERS

More and more individuals have recently been looking to trade as both a type of capital and a type of company. Forex trading or currency trading is rapidly becoming one of today's most common types of equity trading.

And with minimum start-up assets needed, the entry barriers are relatively small, making it simpler for the road person to begin trading on the Forex market.

But unless you're a bank or big financial institution, you'll need a broker's facilities to be prepared to trade currencies.

Fortunately, there is a combined rise in the amount of Forex brokers on the industry, with a rise in supply for FX Trading.

The issue confronting most prospective Forex traders, however, with so many brokers to choose from, is not how to trade but how to pick a credible broker to start trading with.

Unfortunately, not all business brokers are the same. As a trader, you will need to locate an appropriate broker to meet your particular requirements.

And this could demonstrate to be the difficult component from practice, as not all brokers give the same facilities or have the same fees and practices. Slight variations in fees like the distribution of the pip will have a big effect on the upper row of your earnings.

Seriously, you need to concentrate on the economies if you want to create a living as a Forex trader and not care about questionable brokers. Choosing a credible Forex currency trading broker should, therefore, be one of the key objectives that you need to do before you even begin trading.

In fact, there are several variables that create a foreign exchange broker a successful one, and here are my best 10 suggestions for selecting excellent currency trading brokers.

1. Reputation

In this type of business, reputation is essential as there is quite a range of "fly-by-night" activities in the industry. Basically, sticking with the more developed Forex currency trading brokers with an excellent track record is the standard of thumb.

A significant element to remember is that it must be verifiable for all their company transactions. Do they have many fulfilled clients with a lawful department? Have they been in company for many years or have they only appeared tonight?

You can figure out a lot of data about their interactions with brokers from unbiased review websites. If you've torn someone off before, you likely should be steering clear.

Dependable brokers in their transactions and activities should be clear. Relevant data on how they work must be readily accessible internet to enable prospective traders to discover out more about their profile and results easily.

2. Regulations

Whatever nation you reside in, always select a Forex broker who conducts company in a nation where a legislative agency monitors their operations. A credible Forex broker needs to be controlled and responsible to the regulators concerned.

The Swiss banking scheme, for instance, is one of the most tightly run vessels in the globe governed by the Swiss Federal Department of Finance, while US Forex trading brokers should be formal representatives of the National Futures Association (NFA) and enrolled with the Commodity Futures Trading Commission (CFTC) as a Futures Commission Merchant (FCM).

In other phrases, they have to adhere to sector laws and laws and comply with them. The last thing you want is some unregulated broker keeping your cash in the center of nowhere. If they go under, you will always get excellent fortune home your cash.

If no monetary authority regulates a broker, instead it may be easier to pick another broker.

3. Differences In Pip Spread

Currency trading brokers do not pay a premium or deposit, unlike stockbrokers. Instead, they create their contribution from the gap in the currency pair's pip distribution when you trade.

Unlike other financial markets, a key reserve does not trad the currency market, so the significance of this transfer is determined by the broker you use instead.

Most Forex brokers post current or postponed rates on their portals so traders can match variations in distribution, and some brokers even give a range of variable pips.

The idea of a variable distribution may seem appealing at first sight due to the Forex market's volatility. The distribution is fairly low when the industry is silent, but when the industry is really heating up, the range distinction could only widen big enough to wash out your earnings.

Unfortunately, many brokers are called "pot stores" out there. They don't have your greatest stake in mind, and some have been proven to alter to their benefit the stretches around.

The upper row here is to search for FX brokers with set and small pip yields irrespective of how the industry is moving.

4. Speed Of Execution

Actually, when signing up for a trading card, this is something most novice traders rarely realize.

Most brokers post live rates on their trading platform, but the issue is how quickly they can perform the offer when you press the "Buy" or "Sell" key.

Speed of request execution is imperative, especially if you're a scalper trading the 5-minute charts, can't you potentially hang around hoping for another 5 minutes just to verify the order?

Luckily, opening a demo file with the broker and giving them a test drive is the greatest answer to this issue. This will allow you to check the pace of execution of your trading platform.

5. Minimum Trading Account Size

Broker leverages are increasing nowadays to accommodate for the tiny retailer who has restricted assets but likes a bit of Forex intervention.

Micro and Nano accounts are available, but most brokers are offering the two standard trading account sizes, the Standard and Mini account.

The main distinction between a Standard and Mini account is that a Standard account trades in 100,000 parts, whereas a mini account trades only a fifth of that volume or 10,000 parts per batch.

In other phrases, the mini card deals with the periodic card volume in one fifth. This enables you to participate in the periodic fund a quarter of what you'd gain.

6. Margin & Leverage

Margin cards are the foundation of Forex trading, so create sure that you are fully conscious of the broker's contact conditions before you rush to enter a personal trading office, the last thing you want to know is a broker's margin call.

Make sure you are fully conscious of how your broker calculates the premium conditions and does it alter depending on the currency pair traded? Is it fixed at different times of the day or week, or variable?

Take notice that some brokers are offering distinct standard and mini account price specifications, so be careful.

And when it goes to leverage, most traders are acquainted with the 1:100 proportion, but you understand that some currency trading brokers today even give up to 1:400 leverages.

If you're a novice trader, don't use too much leverage as this is one of the main factors why so many newbie traders get washed out so quickly. Remember, compounding tiny, coherent earnings is the secret to gaining the Forex match.

7. Rollover Rates

Rollover prices are fees earned when traders transfer their roles to the next day of trading.

If you're a scalper or day trader, your trading record may not be affected by this level, but if you're a swing trader or a long-term trader, if you're not conscious, this seemingly tiny number may sometimes snowball.

That's why it's essential to figure out the minimum percentage criteria for earning a place overnight? Is it a small 0.5%, or a stunning 2%, go do the numbers.

8. Trading Platform

A successful trading platform should demonstrate not only real live rates allowing traders to "buy" or "sell," but also a number of other characteristics such as mapping and instruments for technical analysis.

Some systems give even more sophisticated features such as drifting starts, portable trading, and even the use of automated trading software called specialist advisors.

Most brokers will have their own proprietary trading platform, but many use the Metatrader 4 platform as it is a relatively easy-to-use scheme that can accommodate all ages of traders from novices to professionals.

In my novel, the sort of trading platform used can either create trading the Forex market a relief or a true hassle, so create sure that by joining up for a demo card, you get a taste of the system.

9. Technical Support

The sort of assistance typically occurs in the form of telephony or email assistance, and in some instances, even "Live Chat."

Since the Forex market is a 24-hour worldwide industry, the associated assistance supplied by the broker should also be available 24 hours a day.

Remember, it maybe 3 pm in the afternoon for you, but it may also be 3 am in the evening for another trader around the globe, so make sure that someone from the broker's department will take up the call if something gets incorrect.

A key element of assistance that needs to be highlighted is the capacity to close an "accessible" stance over the phone in the sad case that your PC or internet connection breaks, be careful, anything can occur if Murphy's law starts in.

10. Additional Value-Added Services

Most of the stronger Forex trading brokers deliver excellent value-added services from their own board of in-house advisors in lieu of free webinars, technical instruments, e-books, journals, and even regular business research.

This may just be useful if you're the sort of trader who's trading basics.

Well, that's my 2 cents worth when it gets to discovering credible Forex trading brokers, hopefully in all your Forex trading enterprises, it will provide you with enough data for a successful head beginning.

SHORT TERM FOREX VS. LONG TERM FOREX TRADING

The Differences

In brief, all forex traders are divided into two different organizations and short-term traders. Knowing the difference between the two is useful when choosing the trading style that best suits you. It is also very essential to know the beneficial elements and the negative to a trading style.

In the beginning, we will look at the beneficial elements of short-term trade. A quick move is the first, the most obvious drawback to short-term strategies. Day trading or market scalping can be a very interesting job once you are lucrative. The attraction of fast-fast cash attracts most newcomers to the market and, therefore, a type of forex scalping approach. Now that fast cash is not only a dream. It's a truth when you know how to scalp. The absence of exposure to the market is another benefit of short-term trading. Positioning is often open only as you stand before the screen and when you leave or switch off the computer. None of the risks is of value to many traders when you leave the computer.

Let's now look at some negative aspects. The high-stress environment of short-term trading is particularly important. Most fresh traders in the forex market often believe they can start with the jump. Without adequate foreign-trade training, most fresh, short-term traders will not understand and often fail to manage the pressure of day-trade. Enormous quantities of time can only conquer the quickly passed price effect of scalping behind the screen, or most effectively by watching the scalper live, which is a lucrative business already. The volatility intra-day is another drawback to short-term policies. This not only affects the transfer period but also prevents the effects of volatility on the drop locations. The wrong stop is going to cost you the trade, even if you have the right track. Although excellent timing is great for long-term business entries and departures, it is not important. It's all approaches in most brief-term!

Long-term Forex trading is more of a purchase and holding strategy. Unlike short-term trade, position traders seek to take advantage of the economy's general direction and may be less interested in volatility every day. Positionings are more often than not based on the direction of the basic currency, as do short-term traders, where technical analysis is usually highlighted. Long-term traders, also called position traders, can only be traders one or two a year. They can look at their situation only once a week or possibly even less than regularly looking at the market. The position trader can be maintained for weeks, months and even a year or longer depending on the length of time needed to make a profit or if things go the wrong direction.

The length of time required for trade is an advantage for forex market trading. You do not have to sit on your desktop every day. Even if you have a full-time job, finding the time to place a trade would be difficult, and keeping the basics takes only minutes per week. That is why longer-term trading is exclusively suitable for daily work or the investor's otherwise busy schedule.

Lack of intervention is a few of the long-term trading drawbacks. If you are an active investor, waiting months for a business to develop is simply not an alternative. Besides, they're always on the market once trades are entered. World events and other unforeseen conditions are compulsory for this position at all times, adequate loss of stops. Position trading also opens up something in the forex market that is called swap. When you buy a currency pair, you sell the second currency in a couple. If the first nations ' currency is not larger, the interest will be paid or swapped.

Above all, any kind of trading's benefits and disadvantages. In this paper, there are only a few. When choosing your business style, you should look at your lifestyle and yourself as an individual. Do you like an active enthusiasm for business? Do you protect capital or the construction of capital? Want to be in front of the screen every day? How much time for your current trading schedule is available? All this is practical in choosing your business style, and as you look at yourself and your timetable, you will see the business style that best suits your character and lifestyle.

Forex Day Trading: 5 Errors To Avoid

In a high-leverage retail forex trading game, there are some practices that could result in a complete loss of capital. Five popular mistakes are made by day traders in an attempt to improve returns, but that has the opposite effect at last.

Five possible terrible mistakes can be avoided by comprehension, discipline, and an alternative approach.

Average Downward Trend

In Forex Traders, the average downward trend is often average. It's rarely intended, but many traders achieved it. It is difficult to average in forex markets. Multiple problems exist.

The main question is the loss of time–not just the sacrifice of money. Therefore, it can be better this time and money.

Secondly, to recover lost capital, it is important to recover your remaining assets from the initial losing trade. If a trader loses 50% of his property, it requires 100% to return him to the original level of capital. Losing enormous amounts of capital on individual trades or on individual trading days can hamper long-term capital growth.

Reducing inevitably leads to major losses or margins because the trend can be longer than the liquidity of a trader— especially if more capital is added as losses take place.

Day traders are susceptible to such issues in particular. The short duration for companies means short-lived opportunities and quick exits for bad companies.

Forex Trades for News

Traders have been noticed by news events that will change the market, although the direction is not previously known. A trader, for instance, can have complete trust in the Federal Reserve's price impact by stating that the media will raise interest prices or not. However, traders can't forecast how the industry will respond. Other variables, such as extra claims or numbers and potential information in media advertisements, may render business motion highly illogical.

Also, as volatility and all kinds of contracts impact the industry, breaks are initiated on both parties. This often leads to whipsawing before a pattern happens (if in the short run, you happen).

That is why standing in front of a message could seriously jeopardize a trader's probability of accomplishment.

Forex Trades after News Hits
While reactionary money is easy and unpretentious, it can be just as catastrophic as a trade if it is accomplished without a powerful trading strategy in an untested way.

Day traders should wait for volatility to decrease and generate a definitive tendency after news reports. This enables liquidity problems to be reduced, a risk to be managed more effectively, and business direction to be stable.

Excessive risk-taking is not equivalent to one percent of capital in forex trading — excessive revenue. In the long run, almost all traders who are risking high capital on individual trades will end up losing their cash. A common rule is that a trader should not risk more than 1% of his property in a single trade (concerning the cost of admission and termination). Professional traders often risk far less than 1% of equities.

Day trade also calls for unique attention in this area, and maximum daily hazards should be implemented. It may be approximately 1% (or less) of assets or the average daily profit over a 30-day period. For instance, under those risk parameters (leverage not included), a trader with an account of 50,000 $could lose up to 500 $a day. This can be altered so that it matches an average daily profit more (that is, the losses are nearly 100 dollars or less if a trader makes 100 dollars during good days).

The method aims to guarantee that the account will not have any significant impact on a single business or trading day. A trader, therefore, understands that they won't lose more than in a single business day or day by taking the risk maximum equivalent to a 30-day average daily profit.

Unrealistic Expectations

There is much to say about unrealistic expectations in Forex Trading, which come from a variety of sources but often lead to all these problems. We often impose our own business expectations on the market but can not hope that they will act as we want them to. In brief, medium-term and long-term cycles of the market are all choppy, volatile, and tendencious. The market is of no importance to any individual desire and traders must agree. Every movement and every profit can not be isolated, which leads to frustration and misconduct of judgment through belief.

To avoid unrealistic expectations, the best way is to develop a trading plan. Do not constantly change the outcome–even a small profit with forex leverage is able to develop. With the expansion of capital over time, the position can be increased to give higher returns or test new methods.

A trader must acknowledge every day, at various intervals, what the market provides. For example, at the start of trading, the markets are more unstable, so that unique open market strategies may not work later in the day. The day can be happier, and you can follow a further strategy. A pick-up could take place in the near future, and a new strategy could be applied. If you can adopt the offered every day, even though it does not align with your expectations, you are better positioned to succeed.

In terms of averaging, traders should not add positions, but should quickly use an already scheduled exit procedure to sell losers. Traders should sit back and watch news notifications in order to decrease their volatility. Risk must be checked, too, without losing more than one trade or day, which could be easily returned to another.

Finally, by adopting what the industry provides you on a specific day, you have to handle demands. Companies are more probable to success in knowing prevalent retrograde behavior in general and ignoring them.

Long-Term Forex Trading Strategies

This chapter discusses the long-term strategy of financial trading, describes best practices, and takes into consideration the variables of important traders. Many internet currency specialists choose day trading, relying on their excitement and ability for profit. But positional traders are probable to produce bigger earnings, also called long-term forex traders.

Long Term Forex Trading

The objective is to produce fewer transactions that produce more profit for individuals. In general, while traders want to generate almost 200 tubes per enterprise, their opportunities are much lower. Traders using this approach must, therefore, be carefully created and possess substantial knowledge before using it.

Long-Term FX Trade Strategies

Identifying a pattern requires blocks or months. In some instances, over a year, retailers have pursued a pattern. Traders purchase on requirements and sell on the basis of statistics using long-term Forex Trading. Speculators like George Soros, for instance, significantly reduced the British pound in 1992.

They were currently skeptical about Britain's ability to maintain fixed monetary rates. The country received 1 trillion GBP from the ERM and Soros on 22 September 1992. Bear in mind that financial events in the UK as well as the United States when trading GBP / USD must be taken into account. The economies of the two currencies should be evaluated as well as the potential for unexpected events.

An Example Of Long-Term Strategy

Some general information on long-term forex trading is provided in the previous section. Look at a long-term strategy more carefully: just say you're a Forex dealer based in the USA, and there have been some political occurrences that are likely affected by US dollars. Use the available information to evaluate the target of the USD.

If you feel the cash will shift according to your forecast, you can begin your long-term forecast trading strategy by opening a US dollar pair position. But believe about where the second currency is going before that. To be conservative, choose a quotation that is most stable, in your opinion.

In your currencies with the Middle East, for example, Japan does not have tight trade agreements with countries in the region, and Japan's yen (JPY) is historically stable. You could feel this is the perfect pair for your trade, the US Dollar / JPY currency pair. You must double-check your expectations and list all knowledgeable expectations and their outcomes when you comprehend them. All of these variables are covered by how you build this, and any other long-term currency trade strategy.

How to Trade Forex Long-term

There are several tips to improve your FX trade. Let your emotions not begin because they can undermine your effectiveness seriously. It may be a challenge to turn losing trades into winner trades, but it may also be difficult to shoot early and lose future profits.

Keep to your strategy, whatever happens. Predict where the currency is going and how large the price move is every time you open up space. You must also ensure that every business has a profit and a stop-loss goal. Along with long-term forex methods, always figure out.

Long-term Trading Best Practices

Although most position traders have different strategies, there are some general guidelines. The guidelines are based primarily on risk management and the inherent nature of the FX industry.

Let's explore how to improve your business strategies:

Use very small leverage
When performing position trading, you should stick to a small percentage of your margin. In long term exchange operations, one of your main variables is to keep your common volatility within, or even during, the week. Because a pair of currencies can move hundreds of pipes easily a day, make sure that these price fluctuations do not cause a stop.

Pay attention to swaps

In the long term, profit is essential as trade-in Forex can generate promising incomes. Be cautious of swaps–the price of overnight stays. Sometimes swaps can be positive. However, in many cases, it is negative to evaluate your costs to make Forex policies workable for long-term growth. Sometimes the piping profit may be low, but the swap is beneficial to you.

Effort vs. Return Ratio

Take into account that even with the best approach, you can't attain your profit objective. This can easily happen if the leverage is too low. If you trade only with small capital quantities, you should expect proportionate returns. Because of this, the time spent on trading in comparison with economic incentives should always be taken into consideration. In most instances, comparatively big sums of capital are required to pay effort vs. the return ratio.

How To Plan An Effective Long-Term Forex Trading Strategy

Large-scale trading is one of the safest methods for the forex business. The big picture is shown with all the available currency pairs information.

Interest rate

You can not ignore interest rates if you want to trade a bigger image. When you maintain currency trading for a day, you will see something called a rollover. Depending on the currencies and direction of your company, you can pay some interest or receive some interest. Most of the moment, international traders purchase the currency in comparison with weaker currencies.

Fundamentals

The above concepts are followed by basic monitoring of financial leadership, also known as the fundamentals. Work, interest rates, CPI, and even politics are fundamental problems. When trading the entire picture, you have to comprehend the fundamentals of the currencies involved.

Technical

When applied, technical analyses have numerous methods. Another market operator may consider MACD when telling a merchant to produce technical, analytical information, and when mentioning technical trading. In the big picture, you are looking for technical components to assist your trade. If you want to buy a currency couple, you don't want it technically overbought. In your grand picture trading, you should have a technical analysis to help you choose. It helps to prevent you from entering a bad time. It allows time for you.

You may have the right idea in general, but technical analyses can reduce your risk.

Like all evaluations, technical analysis may dismiss appropriate investment decisions by mistaken or prejudicial measures.

Weekly charts

If you have no feeling of something happening with a currency pair on a single day, step back and see it all in the weekly diagrams. The bigger weekly diagrams can make the daily diagram trivial and provide you with a more comfortable sensation. A step back helps reduce second thinking.

With these products which assist positions you maintain, you can take strong trading decisions into account. You should never do a company. You could explain to them to a third party if you had to. This enables you to avoid doing trading, which "I'm bored." Actual trading, especially big image trading, can be boring and slow. Many traders were introduced and promptly advised that there are so many ineffective forex traders.

BEST AUTOMATED FOREX TRADING SOFTWARE

You will understand as a forex trader, how complicated trade can be, particularly if anything goes incorrectly. Some businessmen dream of an intelligent partner, who isn't emotionally exposed, who is logical, always seeking lucrative trade, and can almost instantly perform business. If all of these things are looked for, the search could be over as the finest automated trading software for Forex also included in all these characteristics.

Many programs of this sort are easy to access. Your principal job is to operate without the Forex trader by scanning the use of pre-established parameters or intended parameters that are programmed to the scheme by the customer for useful currency transactions. In short, you can switch your PC on with automated software, enable the program, and then go away while trading the software. That is the fundamental principle.

The purpose of this chapter is to provide more data about the automated software components so that you can choose the best automated pre-extraction trading software.

Who Can Use Automated Software And How Does It Work?

Hypothetically, newspapers, professional traders, or experienced Forex traders can use FX trade software to create their trading decisions. The software is effectively accessible at a wide variety of rates, including various sophistication norms for various demands. Online customer reviews of such FX programs reveal their strengths and weaknesses. Most programs offer a free demonstration and other purchase incentives. An additional provider may provide the user with a free demo model.

One of Forex's most beneficial elements is that marketing incentives to purchase particular packages may provide additional instruments for trade. However, the programs are not infallible–and the trader should be conscious that the use of the software does not ensure 100% of good business. Let's see how this software sort effectively functions.

Automated Forex trading software is a PC software that analyses both monetary and market price diagrams. It identifies signals, tracks differences in price and news trends that can influence the market, to find possibly useful currency pairs. For example, the software will use the criteria the user sets, determine a currency pair trade that meets the defined profitability parameters, and also send or buy alerts. With this warning, you can program the software to perform the trade automatically.

The Advantages Of Automated Software In Forex

Although no automated Forex software is recommended, the advantages of it must still be described. One major benefit of identifying what to trade is the removal of emotional and psychological influences. The automated software ensures consistent and completely unemotional trading decisions, exploiting parameters that you previously defined or installed by default.

New and even experienced traders may sometimes trade on the grounds of a psychological trigger that does not conform to the logic of the market. There are no different human judgments with automated trading. In addition, auto forex trading software can be efficient for monetary speculators who do not trade based on the interest rate but rather on a specific currency spread. Due to the immediate obvious price discrepancies, the data is read by the trading scheme, and therefore trade is performed.

Furthermore, other market aspects may cause buying or selling alerts, such as average moving overheads, chart settings (such as triple bonds or heads, or other support or resistance level indicators). Automated software programs also allow traders to simultaneously manage multiple accounts, which is a real plus, which can not be manually operated on a single computer readily.

Automatic software or an automatic Forex trading robot saves substantial time for severe forex traders with other significant interests, jobs, or bonds, which could otherwise have been dedicated to other significant operations such as market surveying, analysis of distinct graphs, or observation of multiple currency price occurrences.

Automated FX trading systems enable the trader to release himself from the computer screen while the program scans the market for trading possibilities-thus trading under correct circumstances. That means that the program is continually in operation day or night and does not need human control. Use Admiral Markets ' free live webinars to know about automated trading systems. There is plenty of practical advice and perspectives for beginners and experienced specialist traders seeking something more in-depth.

Choosing Your Automated FX Trading Program

While not all programs run well on the Internet, you will discover something helpful, perhaps the finest automotive trading software Forex. However, some companies claim that they have an extremely large proportion of profitable businesses. You're supposed to be careful. Such claims must be checked on advertising. Indeed, without a doubt, the finest software publishers provide authenticated trading history outcomes to demonstrate the efficiency of the programs they offer. The golden rule is to recognize that previous achievement does not guarantee favorable outcomes for the future.

Define Your Needs

Since the speed, performance, programming capacity, and the complexity of the automated trading systems vary, what is good for a trader could not be good for another. Some traders in Forex would like a program to produce reports or to impose stops, trail stops, and other specific market orders. In any automated or automated Forex trading robot, effective real-time monitoring is a significant component. Other traders, like beginners or those less experienced, might want a simpler program with a fixed and forgotten function.

Furthermore, if you often travel or want to be away from your PC for a long time, remote access capacity is essential. Thus, your program should provide complete access and functionality through Wi-Fi or any other type of internet access from any present place. The most helpful and helpful technique to serve traders and their requirements can be a web-based program.

It is essential to point out that the prudent Forex dealer has a virtual private server hosting or VPS. VPS service. VPS is sold to various businesses and offers huge quick access, isolates for safety reasons the automated Forex software, and also offers technical support.

Also, some companies tend to pay additional charges and commissions for trading. Other businesses may argue that no charges or commissions are imposed. You can draw up your profitability commissions and charges, so your customer agreement must be thoroughly checked. Furthermore, top companies offer various return guarantee programs. If the client chooses not to be good enough, the prime companies will allow you after purchase to refund the complete reimbursement of Forex automated trading software for some time.

How To Test The Software

Certain businesses supply market video content, acquire or sell software currency pairs. If there are screenshots of business prices for product acquisition and sale, benefit, and execution of the accounts, you should verify them before committing. Driving the training tutorial or other functions while testing fresh Forex automatic trading software to see whether it is suitable and to answer all of your issues. Also, the help desk may have to answer complicated programming questions such as buy-sell criteria and use the scheme generally.

If you have a support connection, check how simple it is to browse, and if it is helpful for you. Some of your issues may not be answered via the assistance and knowledge base data supplied. Often, most of the major companies are also offering their automated Forex trading robots a free, un-mandated test, so that the possible client can see if the program fits well. In such a situation, try to determine if the program can be easily installed and ensure your understanding and use of it is difficult.

Also, make sure the software is flexible and programmed so you can alter any pre-installed default settings.

Main Points To Consider While Choosing Automated Software

Most of the famous auto forex trading software will trad the most volume and liquidity in the major currency pairs. They are USD / EUR, USD / GBP, USD / CHF, JPY. Trading techniques will differ from conservative ones to more adventurous, risky trading strategies, with programs intended to scalp a few points in an industry. The customer chooses which approach to use and can adjust the strategy in each direction.

You should consider reading the internet review of the client item before purchase since it offers a useful source of data on software for automated currency trading. Pricing is currently favorable for the consumer, so perhaps shopping around for the best deal is a good idea, but make sure that quality isn't sacrificed at a price. Trading package prices can vary from hundreds to thousands of dollars. Finally, seek a high level of service and technical assistance. For Forex traders, this is essential at any point of expertise and is particularly important for novices and newbies.

Final thoughts

What level of expertise you have in forex trading doesn't matter. Whether you're a beginner, a trader, or a specialist, Forex automated software can be of assistance. Trading in any industry always presents potential hazards–and the software does the same. On the Internet, there are many scams. Due diligence of any business can prevent fraudulent software.

It is important to realize that no Forex automated software guarantees a 100% winning rate. It is also important to remember that past accomplishments do not guarantee future success.

WHAT ARE FOREX AUTOMATED TRADING SIGNALS AND WHICH ARE THE BEST?

You've probably experienced a number of distinct Forex indicators as a trader. Any beginning Forex trader's main task is to learn how to trade efficiently and attain Forex business understanding, rather than just capturing texts that they may not completely understand. That being said, it is helpful for traders of all skill concentrations to know what those indicators truly imply for a trader in particular and how to execute them.

We will clarify what Forex automated trading sensors are in this section, along with the advantages and prospective risks of using them. We will also provide you with an outline of the facilities supplied by Forex channel suppliers as well as some of the present industry suppliers and what they are offering.

What Are Forex Signals?

First, let's find out what messages are from Forex. Signals function as a currency traders trading warning, notifying traders when to join or leave a trade. Signals can be divided into two separate groups:

- ✓ Fundamental Signal
- ✓ Technical Signals

The first item in the roster is a basic method of Forex waves. Fundamental analysis refers to economic occurrences, corporate announcements, and business media, all of which can affect financial tools ' price motions. A basic message is simply one of those occurrences that a trader can use to create educated trading choices, such as an interest rate announcement.

Traders will need to maintain an eye on media and business announcements to unlock basic messages. They can also use an economic calendar to remain up-to-date with future activities to make sure they're able to behave as quickly as the media stops. Customers can also see emerging information from Dow Jones in the MetaTrader trading platform at Admiral Markets.

While basic analyses weather and financial occurrences, the focus of technical analysis are on historical stock trends and trends of charting. By seeing how tools have worked in the past, traders can forecast how they could act in the future if comparable trends arise.

When a chart pattern shows that the cost of an instrument will shift in a certain path, a technical indicator, using historical information and indices, traders can produce their messages or use Forex drones or subscribe to Forex signal facilities for automatic alerts.

Technical Forex warnings are frequently released in conjunction with various risk management approaches to guarantee that minimal casualties happen if the present scheme does not operate as originally anticipated. Most internet Forex messages appear to fit within this range, which can create a much harder job of searching for the finest Forex trading message supplier.

What Are The Benefits Of Using Automated Forex Signals?

For Forex traders, the benefits of automated Forex signals include:

Save Time
You don't have to waste time creating your own trading strategy. It can be a lengthy method to develop your FX trading strategy so you can choose to follow your own trader with a comparable threat picture. You also save an enormous quantity of moments by putting trades and tracking various economies.

Diversify the risk.
You can pick various FX policy suppliers so that your result is not based on just one strategy's results.

Highlight more opportunities for trade.
If you have a present approach or an EA (Expert Advisor), incorporating automatic Forex sensors can rapidly bring additional approaches to your trading combination.

Save at the fees.
Social trading is an option low-cost to well-known traditional money management.

Low Entry Barriers.
You are not required to have a minimum equilibrium for social trading to start or continue. Anyone with connections to MT4 can do it as a subject of reality.

There is no paperwork.
To begin with printing symbols, there is no complex and frustrating documentation to pass through.

Maintain your account's control.

The account you use for social trading is in your name, so you don't need to offer anybody the lawyer's authority.

You are protected well.
You choose how much to spread to your approach when you decide to follow a trader, and you can put a stop-loss on your MT4 card if they do not execute as you hope.

Share success with you.
Your effective policies can even be shared.

Forex Signal Providers Overview

Forex messages can be acquired from different firms specializing in this system, as well as from a variety of leading Forex brokers providing normal or VIP payments to traders.

It is important to consider that some may offer the service free of charge when you are using a broker, while others may charge between USD 5-10 per day or maybe more. There are bundles with a one time lasting access subscription payment, frequently starting from $100 to $150, but it can be as high as a little amount varying on the source.

Services you benefit from joining up with a supplier of Forex indicators usually vary from company to company. Performance trackers, email, SMS alerts, email or mobile customer support, and, of course, advanced evaluation of more sophisticated deals- because Forex signal delivery suppliers need to safeguard their policies.

Note that some service suppliers will merely provide Forex instructions and give it to the trader to carry out the trading. Other suppliers will be doing the business for you. This trading model includes some confidence behind the published Forex indicators in the selected business or person.

The confidentiality of the web-based alternatives will differ extensively, as in any industry. However, if you find suppliers with achievement levels of 80-90 percent, you should leave those allegations seriously–if it seems too great to be accurate, it is likely. Of course, there are firms with excellent achievement levels, but they will be willing to provide proof and data to substantiate their allegations if they are real.

Keep in mind that your capacity to use the acquired Forex messages effectively relies on the effectiveness of the product provided by your broker. This is particularly valid with news-based Forex trading, where you need to behave as rapidly as feasible, ensuring that any problems linked to slippage and misquotes are minimal.

Whether or not you will use Forex messages will rely on your character and personal business plan. For example, if you are an extremely engaged person with little time to do a thorough market analysis, Forex indicators provide an option for electronic trading. If you want to know the mechanics of trading in-depth, subscribing to MQL5 Forex alerts will give you a very small advantage. The signal implementation relies on your trading skill stage, aspirations, and primary objectives.

Comparing 3 Forex Signal Providers

It is essential to create sure that you have taken the correct choice before subscribing to a paid trading message. With this in mind, by linking some of the best Forex signal suppliers on the industry-MetaTrader, MQL, and ZuluTrade, we have performed some groundwork for you.

Forex Signals In Metatrader

The trading systems MT4 and MT5 provide an extensive Forex signal collection for trading through the embedded MQL5 signal service. You can subscribe to custom or pay offers with a private card or a custom card. It will also be performed on your consideration if the message supplier creates a trade. It is essential to remember that messages are accessible free of charge and charged.

Paid messages are connected to a monthly subscription that can be canceled at any moment. You should be conscious, however, that the service may be charged, so you should closely inspect whether the message is appropriate for you and your approach. For each person trading message, MetaTrader provides comprehensive statistics.

In this summary, you can see significant stats needed for or against a Forex message like:

- ✓ The growth of the signal over the entire period
- ✓ The number of weeks the signal exists
- ✓ The number of subscribers
- ✓ The maximum decrease in percent and the profit factor
- ✓ The subscription costs

Of course, choosing a message that has persisted for a long time and has continuously been successful creates meaning. So here you can do the original processing. You will obtain extra extensive statistics on that message when you tap on a message. You will see a sign on this screen, and you will obtain statistics on the signal's most significant parameters. Here you can create your final selection as it collects all the data.

For instance, you can utilize the curve and several statistical reports to evaluate the signal risk you see trading, trading tools, and choose when the forex signal is right for you. In the beginning, you even have the option of displaying all trades directly in a graph with the' Visualization' button.

MQL Signals

MQL5 is a traders group that uses MetaTrader 4 and MetaTrader 5, set up by MetaQuotes-the MetaTrader designer. While the MetaTrader system contains a variety of sensors, MQL5 provides traders with exposure to a broad spectrum of sensors created by others in the society that can assist satisfy a variety of trading requirements.

To allow Forex transmissions, you merely need to sign up for a group username for MQL5 and then register it in your FX trading platform environments.

As you can see, the MT4 scheme has many benefits. Importantly, MT4 Forex self-trading emails do not require you to change brokers as the suggestions are instantly in your current MT4 department. Also, you will have a similar allocation as you do with a normal deposit. By expanding the allocation, you will be paid by other email providers.

Not only can this benefit you much more per trade, but you will most probably have less successful trades over a lengthy span of a moment. Finally, as there are millions of MT4 consumers around the globe, you have links to the MT4 society. You can plug into the enormous current MT4 foundation of traders and specialist consultants.

ZuluTrade

ZuluTrade is a famous network of social trading and an online site for Forex trading. It is open and available to all internet consumers and provides a secure working demo account. This openness implies that everybody on this network can become a trader or a' message supplier' of automatic Forex trading devices. There is a huge amount of frequency suppliers-over 10,000-that you can scan for according to your desires.

Users also have links to a results chart in which ZuluTrade ranks all service suppliers according to their achievement level. Ranking can be a good beginning point, but be careful. We've seen more than one of these frequency providers occur in the top five within a specified month, creating only a large reduction and falling out of the ultimate ZuluTrade ranking graph of the next month. You can display a variety of efficiency indices and charts for each service supplier to assist you in assessing them. ZuluTrade is completely transparent about historical entry and data about every single trade that consumers have done in the past. Within Microsoft Excel, you can tap all historical trades to create your assessment. Looking for reliable and coherent message suppliers requires some expertise and frequent good tuning, particularly if you are looking for the finest integrated Forex transmissions. You can use a wide variety of brokers in ZuluTrade. The U.S., UK, Russia, and New Zealand have over 50 sponsored brokers.

The advantages of ZuluTrade are:

- ✓ A free functioning demo trading account, so that you can try it out without spending money.
- ✓ An extremely wide choice of traders or so-called signal providers to follow or copy.
- ✓ A choice of brokers in different countries.

- ✓ Data is open for users and is fully transparent.
- ✓ Customers may comment directly on profile pages of signal providers.
- ✓ Low ongoing cost.
- ✓ No entry cost included and low minimum deposit requirements.
- ✓ Money management features.
- ✓ Good mobile apps.

However, there are some drawbacks:

- ✓ There are more poor and inconsistent signal providers than there are successful ones.
- ✓ Signal providers are not obliged to trade using their own money.
- ✓ For non-FX traders or beginners, money management can be rather difficult.
- ✓ It requires regular monitoring until the right mix of signal providers is selected.

Overall, ZuluTrade is an excellent social trading platform with small continuing expenses and a network stripped of entry costs. Simple knowledge of money management is nevertheless required.

We addressed Forex symbols in-depth in this section, identifying what they are, their kinds, and their overall Forex trading implementation. Our purpose is not to pick a particular message for you, but rather, if you want to include hints in your trading strategy, to give you an idea of what is accessible.

Remember, though many advantages may seem to give hints, they are not a substitute for knowledge and trading abilities. Build your knowledge and understand the Forex trading industry properly before you begin relying too strongly on indicators.

WHY YOU HAVE TO START FOREX TRADING

Why do you think about foreign or forex trading? It's big business, and almost $2 trillion is traded every day because it's a convincing reason. For the informed trader, the potential to make cash is there. The world's biggest forex market. Its amount of trading is greater than the American stock market and greater than all of the global stock markets combined.

8 Reasons For Forex Trading

Trading overseas currencies (Forex trading) have a few major benefits compared to trading shares. Eight motives for trying FX trading where stated below.

1. Trading Forex 24hrs Every Day

Stocks are traded in the stock market. These bonds are available only during ordinary operating hours, usually, from 9 am to 5 pm.

Forex trading is distinct: during nearly six days a week, you can trade currency pairs around the clock. So "operating" as an FX trader is completely up to you. Theoretically, you can do this 24 hours a day. You can do it in the afternoon (before you go to function with your business) or in the afternoon after your regular job. Or–you can work whenever you like–when you're an FX trader earning your money.

However, the trading amount is not similarly spread over a day. Currency pairs, such as the Yen, are obviously mainly traded when Japanese traders operate in Japan-that is, early in the morning or at night in US time.

You don't theoretically have to live on your PC. For example, the AvaTrade Forex broker supports Metatrader, which trades automatically.

2. Forex Trading – Anywhere

An Internet device is all you need to do in order to trade FX. From your workplace, from your living room to your home on the veranda, from your company office, or from your beach during a stay in the Bahamas, you can almost trade foreign currencies from all over the world. And with a web trading program, from everywhere on the world you have a mobile data connection, you can trade with Windows Mobile from your mobile device or your iPhone. Forexyard has created an iPhone app, and try it out now! The proven Forex Broker

3. Liquidity in the FX Market

The foreign currency market is the world's most liquid market. That means buyers and sellers match in a fraction of a second. The daily volume (number of shares traded daily) for trading a small börse is small if you want. Liquidity in the Forex market is very high as the volume of daily trade exceeds US$ 4 trillion.

Due to the market size, there are two other great advantages, in addition to liquidity: low risk of price manipulation and low trading costs. Price manipulation by some participants on the market is almost impossible, given the liquidity and size of the market. To manipulate exchange rates, you need enormous amounts. And because there is such an enormous spread of the market between buying and selling rates. The more liquid a market, the lower the trading expenses. And the reduced the trading costs. The reduced the price to attain a profit.

4. No Commissions in Forex Trading

Unlike trading in stocks, when you buy or sell currencies with a broker, you do not have to pay any commissions. The only "cost" that occurs is the distribution. Your FX broker makes money from you with every trade that you create the tiny variation between the purchase price and the selling price (the bid spread) for most traded currency pairs, usually below five pipes.

5. Leverage in Forex

You can make large profits (or losses) with very tiny investments with the application of leverage. Common leverage is between 1:50 and 1:1000 for Forex trading. Most of the FX agents give a 1:200 levy on the EUR / USD couple for the most traded currency. By leveraging 1:200, you can move 200 dollars by investing just 1 dollar. Or selling just $100,000 in $500. You double your investment to $1,000 if your currency pair rises by half a percent. Using leverage, you can move enormous quantities of cash with a tiny fraction of your investment. In order to make a profit, the higher the leverage, the less the price motions have to be. And the higher the leverage, the reduced the margin demand. The margin is 0.5%, with a leverage rate of 1:200. This is only $500 in the above example. Your position will usually be automatically sold when it is down by $500 to $99.500 because it is not your margin anymore.

6. Earning money with Forex money in falling markets

If you purchase stock, you expect the value to rise. This will make money for you. Each stock's output depends strongly on the general market's performance. In most cases, the correlation is greater than zero (positive correlation) and even closer to zero in similar and highly related markets (like European Union markets). Therefore, it is quite hard to earn money when buying stocks in an economic downturn.

The market in Forex is totally different in this respect. For instance, you are trading a currency pair with the yen. You only have to look at how the two currencies are developing: what currency against the other currency will enjoy? What currency is going to depreciate? If you believe that the euro decreases against the yen, sell euro (short for euro) and purchase yen for (long for yen). You gained cash when your prediction was right: the yen that you had purchased is now worth more than previously.

FX Trading would be a full zero-sum game if no spreads occurred: What the customer wins for a monetary couple (loss), its counterpart loses (wins). Usually, this is different when shares are purchased: an investor creates a strategic equity ratio and picks stocks to achieve this quota. He will attain gains in increasing markets— the only issue is, with the specified dangers, whether he makes the highest profit.

7. Forex Trading: Simple yet Complex

At first glance, the Forex market looks very easy. The trading quantity is mostly traded in a few currency pairs. The biggest currency couple is USD / EUR. But a set of factors, ultimately affecting certain currencies ' availability and request, determines the swap prices themselves. As the demand for currency increases, rates will increase until the balance between supply and demand is resumed. This method takes place almost every second on the ultra-liquid forex market. The FX industry is simply much more complicated than it appears at first sight; it needs a lot of understanding, time, skill and responsiveness to make a living as a Forex trader. Without high-speed Internet access and automated business programs, a casual merchant is hard to compete in skilled traders.

8. Forex Professional Software for Private Traders

However, professional instruments are already common for FX traders. Even the normal trading or trading software in a web browser enables graphs and other analytical instruments to be used. Great benefits of limiting losses are automated stop-loss orders and revenues when prices have increased sufficiently.

UNDERSTANDING FOREX MARKET ANALYSIS

First of all, only two forces–offer and demand–move the market. For any financial, political, social, science, cosmic, and market case, they are the prevalent denominator. Any world market relies on them - and bulls and bears, together with their open roles, have great significance.

We will discuss the methods, styles, methods, and strategies in this section. Interestingly enough, they all share one thing–they all try to assess supply and demand. Some of them may even be very precise but almost always lag behind the cost. Some others are not going to be very accurate, as financial theories are used in basic forex assessment.

By altering their feelings at distinct moments from bulls to bugs, traders can only generate the market that they are analyzing and then alter it once they start up a fresh business. You must know that you can only achieve a competitive edge over a new trader through the finest Forex supply and demand analysis.

Technical Tools

The only characteristic defining the technical Forex market analysis is that a graph characterizes it. You carry out technical FX assessment if you look at diagrams for any reason. The Dow theory, written by the infamous Charles Dow, offers the logical basis for analyzing the charts. Dow stated, among other things, that the market offers everything. Put, Dow stated that whatever factor has an effect on supply and demand will inevitably be reflected in the price that appears on price graphs in real-time.

Actually, sheer technical assessment calls for almost anything outside the price chart to be investigated, because it contains quantified, unreliable information. This short introduction to Forex technical analysis shows its greatest constraint-it analyses the market's considerations already. The larger issue for business people to consider here is: How can I be competitive if common knowledge is what I understand?

Trading With A Demo Account

Traders are also able to trade without risk with a demonstration trading account. This implies that traders can prevent their assets from being jeopardized, and they can choose to relocate to live markets.

Price Action

Action Price is a subculture that is increasingly common within the technical analysis in Forex since the Forex trade is accessible to masses. This increase in popularity is because while the pricing action is in line with the basic postulate of the theory of Charles Dow, the majority are deemed unable to provide the trader with any competitive edge, as are the classic technical indices.

Price action dealers draw findings from' naked' graphs that support their main choices in information development with price movements. Everything else is there to help, even if deemed, but not to launch trade. The basis for the price-action trading shows that, due to the remaining supply or demand still available, the market often reviews price levels where it has earlier reversed or consolidated.

What Is Remnant Supply And Demand?

Instead of pursuing the market, banks, hedge money, and multinationals institutional traders are only taking care of their orders at the cost they wished. Their forex assessment focuses on where the market will be next or next month. If the market leaves its current amount of trading, your orders will not be canceled. They are open until the market comes back.

The remaining open orders distort the fabric of the market, which attracts the revisit price. This is analogous to how mass distorts and attracts more mass from the material of moment and space. In the daily forex assessment, price action strategies are most commonly employed.

Charting

The graphic is a sequence of price quotes. They give you the recorded market history. We have a cost on the 0Y axis and moment on the 0X axis. The price action itself is presented on the ground. Everything begins with charting regardless of the trading style chosen–long-term position or short term intraday.

Charting itself in the Western world is a comparatively fresh method. The graphs on Wall Street have only been in use for a little more than a decade, though papers in the Far East contain prices of 300 years in the form of candlesticks. These are referred to as "rice price quotes."

Candlesticks are a technical trader's most fundamental instrument. An approach is in itself the use of bare candlestick motifs to predict price movements.

Apart from studying popular models, the fundamental forces of supply and demand that form them should be understood. In addition to learning naked candlesticks, technicians may also use charts. Support and resistance routes, trend routes, triangles, and flags are the most common. Many others are there too. It is essential to recognize that it does not predict future market shifts by promoting structures.

They are only available for a dealer's comfort and their knowledge of the previous movements. The same graph may appear to consist of a range of patterns in various traders, or maybe even the same trader, generating conflicting signals at distinct moments. That is why buildings should not be the main argument in your decision-making, and maybe why supply and demand should.

Technical Indicators

You've definitely seen a technical indicator before when you opened your trading platform. Let us split them into two large groups-trend indices and oscillators. To make them clear.

The trend indicators— moving averages (MA), MACD (moving average divergence), ADX (meaning management index), or Ichimoku — points to trend direction (but not always price direction) and to trend power. The MACD indicators are not always the direction of present price action.

Specializing in oscillators— the RSI Indicator, the Stochastic, or the SAR Indicator— shows the turnover.

In trend economies, trend indices operate well, while in different countries, oscillators operate well. They do it theoretically, at least. A few more, like the Bollinger Bands, are in between. You are using both an MA variation to monitor the trend and the price range channel to indicate the turnarounds.

Lastly, there are indicators based on quantity. These are interesting, as while the trading quantity was always used to define supply and demand in financial trading, it is not possible to measure correctly on the forex spot market. The reason is that Forex is an over-the-counter (OTC) market.

For the absence of a better term, the technical indicators are imperfect. They lag behind the cost, which is often redrawn on the closing of the box. They are frequently used in complementary combinations; otherwise, they fail. And when professional traders advise beginner traders to keep their charts clean and easy, they don't abuse techniques. Finally, trade strategies purely based on technical indicators, can not offer a competitive edge.

Fundamental Tools

Basic analyses of FX markets do not use price charts, but rather financial information such as interest rates, inflation rates, or trade equilibrium ratios. The principle behind the main assessment is that markets may, in the brief term, misprice a monetary instrument but will always ultimately reach the "right" price. A trade chance is then established for the period of this' mispricing.'

Basic FX trade assessment is hardly a way to provide accurate points for entry or departure. However, it is an excellent instrument to predict long-term price changes if it is used knowingly. The fact that, while nations are much like businesses, currencies are not exactly like stocks are the catch with purely financial fundamental elements.

The financial health of a company is directly applicable to its inventory cost. But improved economic performance in countries doesn't necessarily equal growth in the comparative value of their currency. Indeed, the comparative value of a currency is a function of several variables, from domestic monetary policies to financial indicators, technological developments worldwide, global developments, even natural disasters.

Economic Theories and Raw Data

In addition to the feeling of the market, there are several economic theories that operate to locate disparities in the present price and "real" value of a currency. Some examples here: Purchases Power Parity (PPP)-assumes that after adjusting the currency rate, the products should cost identically. If they do not, they offer themselves excellent business possibilities.

Interest Rate Parity (IRP)-basically the same as the PPP, except that in this case, products are economic assets and should produce the same after the interest rate adjustment in separate nations.

The theory of Balance Payment (BPP)–is a trade balance for a country. The domestic currency will depreciate if more products and services than exports are imported.

The Model Definition Real Interest Rate (RIRDM)–the same as IRP. An interest rate-higher currency will enjoy the less appealing investment against the currency.

Model Asset Market (AMM)-similar to the trade balance but measures of foreign investment flows and outflows. The more foreign investment, the greater the appreciation of the domestic currency.

In addition to the above-noted theories, the weekly Forex analyses also contain raw domestic economic data. The information provided may have short-term effects on the market on their publishing: employment information, interest rate, inflation, GDP (Große Domestic Produkt), trade balance, retail sales, durable goods, and other indicators.

Sentiment-Based Approach

This is potentially the easiest way to measure supply and demand other than through cost measures, although it is not unlimited. The technique relies on open interest measurement (open trade), which is the key to demand and supply. This is an idea created by the inventory market: whereby the chances are that the market will change, as amounts of trade increase while open interest decreases.

The Forex spot market is traded over the counter, so it is difficult to track the trade quantity or measure open interest. The' Traders Commitment ' report for the Forex futures market helps traders to assess market sentiments. This has only two issues: First, the quantity of the Forex future is just $100 billion a day compared to the $1.5 trillion spot market of Forex.

Second, there are not only speculators among the most effective traders; there are also hedges that trade in a totally distinct and opposed manner. For example, speculators are selling harder on a strong bullish trend when they buy harder.

Most traders have a tendency to employ strategies for them, be they technical analysis, basic analyses or a blend of the two. There is no doubt that traders can demonstrate the larger image at interest rates, rate of inflation, balances of trade, market feelings, and other fundamentals. In the brief term, however, currencies rarely move in a straight line, meaning that many short-term cost measures are available. Technical analysis can be highly efficient in this field.

Whatever kind of assessment you are using, trace your logic back to the business theory of supply and demand. Go for it, if it is still meaningful. Think some more, if it doesn't.

WHAT IS STOP-LOSS IN FOREX TRADING?

This section discusses different subjects related to stopping losses, including what is an end loss? How can you stop losing? And how important are stop-losses? This paper also gives traders some great approaches with Forex stop losses to make sure they make the most of their business experience.

What Is A Stop-Loss?

A stop loss is an order you make with your FX broker and CFD Broker to sell a safety at a certain cost. To decrease trader loss in a safety situation, a stop-loss order has been created. It's good to have this tool when you can't sit and track yourself in front of the computer. This section explains why a loss stop is required, how it should be set up, and how traders can use some examples of stop-loss approaches.

Why Are Stops Important?

The first logical issue to answer is: what is a halt in the exchange market? In order to recover, a stop-loss is an order placed with your broker to sell a safety at a certain cost. Also, a stop-loss order will mitigate the loss of a security position on the part of an investor. Although most traders associate stop-loss orders with a long position, a short position may also be used.

An order for stop-loss removes feelings that can affect trade choices. This can be particularly useful if the position can not be viewed. For many reasons, stop-loss is critical in Forex. There's, however, one simple reason to stand out–the exact future of the Forex market can not be forecast by anyone. It does not matter how strong a configuration is, or how much information a particular trend could indicate.

The market is unknown about future prices, and any trading entered is a danger. With most popular monetary pairings, FX traders can win over half the time, but their cash management is too poor to lose cash. Failure to manage cash can have an unpleasant result. To avoid that, you should be able to calculate Forex stop loss.

Stop-Loss: Setting Static Stops

Forex dealers may stop at a static cost, with an expectation that stop-loss will be allocated, and they will not move to or change the stop until a stop or limit price is reached. Moreover, due to its simplicity, the ease of this stop system means that traders can indicate that the retribution ratio is at least 1:1 danger.

We are now giving an illustration of how to use Forex stop-loss. Imagine a swinger in Los Angeles that takes up positions during the Asian session with the hope that volatility would have the greatest impact on his business at the European or North American meetings. This trader wants to offer his businesses sufficient space to operate without giving up too much capital if they are mistaken.

Therefore, they put a static stop of 50 pipes at every place. They want to set a take-up rate at least as big as the stop range, and therefore a minimum of 50 pipes will be set in each limit order. If the trader wants to set a 1:2 reward-bearing risk ratio for each item, it can simply put a static stop at 50 pipes and a static ceiling of 100 pipes for each item he starts with.

Static stops can also be based on indices, and you should consider learning how to use stop loss in forex trading if you want to know. Some FX traders take static stops one step further, based on a technical indicator, like the Average True Range, the static stop distance. In addition, FX traders use real market details to assist set this stop, which is the main advantage.

We have had a static stop of 50 pipes with a static limit of 100 pipes in the last instance. But what does 50 pip stop in a volatile and quiet market imply? 50 pipes can be a huge step in a quiet market. When the market is unstable, these 50 pipes can be seen as a tiny step. In addition, using an indicator such as the true average range, price swings, and even pivot points, forex traders are able to use the latest market data to analyze their risk management options more appropriately. It is essential, therefore, to learn how Forex trading can stop loss.

Stop-Loss: Trailing Stops

Static stops can give a major advantage to the strategy of the fresh trader. But other FX traders have taken further steps to maximize the management of their funds. Trailing stops are stops that are adapted to reduce further the downside risk of a trade being incorrect when the trade moves to the trader's favor.

Imagine the EURUSD currency pair being a trader with a pip stop at 1,3150 and 100 pipes with a limit of 1,3300. The trader may envisage adjusting their stoppage from a starting point of 1.3150 to 1.3200 if the trading is up to 1.3250. A trailing end simply puts the stop loss on its entry rate or on the break-even price to safeguard the profits made from their original position, so that if the EUR / USD currency pair is retroactive and moves against the trader.

The breakdown allows the trader to remove the original danger in its trade and can choose to place this risk at another FX trade chance or otherwise maintain that entire amount of risks off the table and settle for the lengthy EUR / USD traded with a safe position. It is an error, not to mention the vibrant stop-loss trailing in forex trading. There are many trailing stops, and dynamic trailing stops are the simplest to execute.

With it, the stop for each 1 pip that the trader favors is adjusted. Accordingly, if the euro / USD currency pair from 1.3200 initial input moves up to 1.3201, the stop will be adjusted to 1.3151 by reference to the above examples.

For traders who want the most control, the trader can manually move stops as the situation moves for them. This could, for instance, be quite helpful for traders whose strategies are focused on trends or rapidly moving markets, since prices play an important role in their general attitude to trade. These traders need to understand how to make a Forex stop loss.

Stop-Loss Strategies

A stop-loss strategy for forex trading is strongly recommended. As soon as you have mastered the ability to determine key levels, you can set the price action strategy, use an adequate risk-reward ratio, and use confluence for your benefit, an effective strategy for stop-loss FX is necessary to move your business to the next level.

You must find the best Forex stop loss strategy for you.
Some examples of stop-loss strategies that you can use are here:

Stop-Loss Strategy: Inside Bar And Pin Bar

In the bar and pin bar trading strategies, we are now going to discuss in detail, so that you know them. With regard to the original positioning of a stop loss, it relies on your trade approach. Although the stop-loss can be set according to your individual preferences, some suggested stop-loss sites exist.

With regard to the pin bar approach, your stop loss should be put behind the pin bar's tail. Whether a bearish or a bullish pin bar does not matter. Therefore, the pin bar trading arrangement will become invalid if prices hit the stop-loss. With that in mind, you should never believe the price that hits the loss as bad. The industry only informs you that there was not enough pin bar configuration.

The Forex Trading Stop loss approach in the bar has 2 choices where a stop loss can be made in contrast to the pin bar approach Stop Loss. It is either high or low behind the bar or high or low behind the bar. Behind the mother, the bar is the most frequent and safest placement of a stop-loss bar.

Again, the interior bar trade configuration becomes invalid if the price reaches your stop loss there. This positioning is safer merely because you have more buffers, which are particularly helpful in hoppers, between the stop-loss and the entry because with this buffer, you can remain much longer in trade.

The second stop loss positioning for the inside bar has to be clarified now - it is up or down behind the inside bar. Because this positioning offers a better risk / reward ratio, traders can use this. The primary pitfall is, however, that it will make you stop before the establishment of the trade has had an opportunity to play in favor of the trader.

This is the riskier choice for this approach for the stop-loss of Forex, the less a buffer between the stop-loss and the input is for a trader. What loss stops to use relies on your own risk tolerance, risk-reward ratio, and currency pairs. Since you understand where the stop loss should be originally situated, we can now examine further stop-loss approaches that you can apply as quickly as the industry moves in the right direction.

"Set And Forget" Or 'Hands Off' Stop-Loss Strategy

The second instance is" set and forget" or" hands-off" of a nice FX Stop Loss approach. You simply place your halt and then let your market go; it's the way. The key principle can not be any simpler. The stop-loss strategy' Set and Forget' alleviates the risk of stopping too soon by keeping your stop loss at a secure distance.

Moreover, this approach helps to remove emotion from your trade because after it is established, it does not require communication. You let the market do the remainder when you're in the trade and stop-loss set. The last benefit is that it can be implemented extremely easily and needs only one intervention.

Of course, this approach has its drawbacks. The greatest and often most expensive inconvenience of this approach is the highest acceptable risk from start to finish. If you risk some cash, you are actually likely to lose the sum from the moment you join the business until you leave.

In addition, your capital can not be further protected. The second trick is that a stop-loss approach' Set and Forget' or' Hands Off' can make you move your stop-loss. Leaving the stop order in one location is even the most knowledgeable trader emotionally challenging. This is likely not the best approach for forex stop-loss, but it still needs your attention.

Stop-Loss Strategy: The 50% Stop-Loss

Although this approach requires half of the danger, it does not exactly have to behalf. The benefit is that we start using the market to let us understand how much assets we have to protect. On a pin bar configuration, traders can use the 50% approach. Imagine a daily close or a market admission with a bullish pin bar. The market ends a bit higher the next day than your entry.

You can now use the low day to conceal your losses instead of even break or closing. Once the market closes the second day following your entry, you can conceal the losses from the low. This allows you to reduce your risk by more than 50 percent, but still takes advantage of the low pricing rate of the past day.

Along with other issues about stop-loss you could have had. It's not difficult to understand why a halt is important, and most business traders understand that they need to stop. In addition, movements in the market can be rather unpredictable. Stop-loss is one of the instruments that FX traders can use to avoid the destruction of a single business.

You should now be able to tell where you can stop losing your future businesses and be aware of the kinds of approaches that you also have.

FOREX TRADING BENEFITS

Forex is for foreign exchange or currency trading. It is a global, highly liquid economy with a huge quantity of periodic trade. As with many acquisitions, for the heartless or unfamiliar trader, Forex trading is not.

Trading in Forex has always been prevalent, although many switches to traditional stocks and trading in shares. Trading forex overstocks, however, has many benefits, including its large earnings capacity without some of the stock market constraints. The reality that forex is a business of 24 hours implies that tiny shareholders who are just beginning out have a wonderful benefit. It implies you can suit your other regular tasks with forex trading-you can even operate on it in the center of the evening if you want! Somewhere around the globe, there is always a bank accessible to trading.

For beginners, Forex trading is also highly simple to get involved in. This is because forex trading charges are usually smaller than when trading stocks and the scheme enables you to practice marginally. This implies that with only a tiny payment, you can purchase large quantities of currency-though this obviously brings both danger and advantages.

Forex operations are usually very fast owing to the reality that money is used for all operations. When you start trading with forex, you'll rapidly start learning how to make effective projections. This is produced easier because learning about the significant currencies is much easier than learning the stock market ins and outs.

This is only a very short summary of the advantages of forex trading. As you can see, for beginners who have little investment knowledge, many of these highlights create it a good option.

If you decide where to trade, then look at the fundamentals of forex, and you may find it to be the perfect choice for you.

Usually, internet Forex trading is performed through a Forex broker. An online trading platform is a broker that provides currency pairs to traders that they can purchase and distribute. It's a question of confidence to select a broker, and the traders need to gather data about the broker before choosing the correct one for them. The cash they spend is one issue traders have. They are worried about how their cash is being put, and if they want to borrow from the broker, they are ready to get their cash home. It is a justification for why collecting broker data and reading about their cash laws is essential. Usually, information is discovered on their blog and on the Internet, where traders share interactions with personal brokers.

In this section, the mindset is the benefits of internet Forex trading.

Market Hours

The business is available 24 hours a day, 5 days a week, as the competition is made up of the entire country. The industry is divided into four sectors: New York, London, Sidney, and Tokyo. Throughout the days, they are open at different times; it means that when the London market closes, the New York market is still open; when the New York market closes, the Tokyo market will open, and the Sydney market will open an hour later. The market in Tokyo will close an hour earlier than the market in Sidney; once the market in Sidney closes, the market in London will reopen.

Leverage

Brokers give power to traders; it implies traders with a tiny quantity of cash can trade with a larger quantity. If a broker offers a 50:1 leverage, traders can trade as they make 50 percent more money than they do. If a trader has 200 Euros and trading with a 50:1 leverage, he will have a 50x 200 Euros currency quantity of 10,000 Euros.

Low transaction costs

Brokers give small or no transaction costs as transaction costs are included in the rates. It is called the spreading rate between buying and selling. An instance is the euro / USD's most traded currency pair; the split is 2 pips in some brokers. It implies that traders must first earn 2 pips before they obtain a profit from a EUR / USD trade. Another example is the GBP / USD currency pair, where at a lot of brokers, the spread is 4 pips. It implies that traders must first earn 4 pips before they obtain a profit from a GBP / USD trade. As the data show, the currency pair-based allocation is one of the variables of why EUR/USD is the most traded currency couple.

Access

The market for forex trading is available 24/5 (24 hours a day, 5 days a week), giving traders more business opportunities than in the future, where future trade usually is only about seven hours a day available. Instead of waiting for the market to open the next day, forex traders can do immediate trading; this aspect of forex trading makes the market more liquid (i.e., closest to cash). Forex is also an incredibly quickly increasing sector, and the exchange of cash on weekly grounds considerably exceeds that of the futures market.

No trading commission

In the futures market, traders are required to send their broker a committee or brokerage premium for all future transactions in which they are involved. There are no trade orders in the forex. Forex brokers create cash through spreading (the distinction between the present cost of the offer and the present cost of the request).

Forex trading takes place not in one place but via the internet and networks but in some significant trading centers around the globe. Foreign exchange brokers operate from their desks via a microphone that is straight attached to a telephone line. The speech of the brokers is continually passed on to the voices of the companies. You can visit http:/www.forexvoice.com to think easier how this is accomplished, and brokers will catch you calling bidding and tender rates. Currencies in combinations such as EUR / USD are cited. Trading in forex means purchasing one currency and distributing another at the same moment. The citation for selling the basic currency is shown on the right and is the amount you can buy. The selling citation is also called the bidding cost of the market maker.

Forex is very liquidity

The big amount of traders in the foreign exchange market and their variety leaves forex distinctive. The currencies that form the foundation of the forex market can be affected by a multitude of variables and are therefore more likely than any other financial market to be subject to speculation on the industry. While the forex market has small profit margins compared to other fixed-income economies, its high amounts of trading enable significant earnings.

Forex Trading Times And Geographical Dispersion Are Unique

Trades for almost 24 hours a day on Sundays between 17:00 EST and 4:00 EST Friday. When it's easy for them, a trader can choose to trade. You can even use auto-trading on numerous trading systems.

Another feature of the Forex industry is the absence of a key legislative authority.
Some nations have their retailers regulated. You only have to deal with controlled retailers. Otherwise, one day, you may wake up and learn that your distributor has taken your deposit!

Forex Offers The Chance To Trade Leverages, Hence Increased Profit Or Loss.

Margin may be used in the inventory market to attain a 2:1 yield, while a 100:1 or 500:1 leverage in the forex market is possible.

To begin trading, you can pick up an account with $25.
You can register your demo file with most brokers and dealers, without charging a fee for as soon as you want.

Free Real-Time Citations Are Available And Advanced Forex Charts.

One instance is Metatrader, which you can freely access with loads of technical tests and specialist consultants to demonstrate to you how to trade forex.

The advantages of foreign exchange trading are important and allowing fresh traders to enter the industry on a monthly basis.

Benefits Traders should, however, combine those advantages with certain risks.

A 24-hour exchange can also imply a brief step can take you if the display is not viewed as occurred during Asian trading hours in October 2016, as the British Pound snap collision. Most of the West did not look at the industry at that moment. High liquidity is accessible on most industries if you need it least, and when you need it most, liquidity can be rare. The liquidity shortage takes place because those who try to complete the trade are sometimes unsure about the rates and typically mistaken to give you a worse cost. While transaction costs are very small when trading in the foreign exchange market, you should be aware that there is not always a stronger trade. Traders may still profit from a larger, less effective approach that would enable them to profit most from Forex's small price design. The grip allowable can be a twin weapon that carries as much risk–if not more risk–as the advantages of leveraging. Leverage feels great when a feature works for you, but often if you don't intend to come out of a trade dropping, it will create matters worse. Profit opportunities due to increasing and dropping rates is an intense advantage, as the obstacle to short-sales in other industries in the Forex market is not seen. However, a simple industry for a short time can create it much easier for a trader to depend on a route and lose confidence that the industry will eventually revert to his advantage.

As on any other industry, trade forex holds a serious threat, which must be grasped, with its solely elevated benefit capacity. Only if good training is achieved can the structure and types of forex be familiarised, the principles of currency price formation, price changes factors, and the level of trading risks and the management of money be successful. In order to address all these variables, you also need outlets of data. Techniques are required in order to evaluate or forecast business motions and trading instruments and regulations.

QUESTIONS ABOUT CURRENCY TRADING

While FX is the largest economic market in the world, retail traders are relatively unfamiliar to it. FX was primarily the domain of significant financial institutions, multinationals, and hedgebanks until internet trading became popular. But moments have changed, and distributors are looking for forex information now.

Whether you're an FX novice or just need to refresh your currency trading abilities, here are the answers to some of the FX industry's most prevalent problems.

1. How Do We Compare Forex To Others?
Currency trading does not take a position on regulated markets and is not controlled by a Central Administrative Body, unlike stocks, futures, or alternatives. There are no clearing houses for trading, and there is no arbitration committee to adjudicate disputes. All respondents trade with each other in credit agreements. In the world's largest, most liquid sector, business is fundamentally only a metaphoric handshake.

At first look, this unique arrangement confuses shareholders used to organize transactions like the New York Stock Exchange (NYSE) and the Chicago Mercantile Exchange (CME). This is an ad hoc deal. But this scheme actually works. Self-regulation provides effective business regulation because both FX competitors have to contend and work together. Furthermore, well-known American retail FX retailers become part of the

NFA, and FX retailers embrace binding arbitration in the event of a dispute in the United States. Therefore, it is critical that any retail client contemplating trading currency does so only through a subsidiary business of the NFA.

The FX industry varies from other economies in other distinguishing ways. Traders who think that the EUR / USD may be dropped may decrease the number of individuals. As stocks do, FX does not have an uptick rule. There are also no limitations to your place's magnitude (as in the past). Thus, in principle, if a trader has sufficient equity, he can buy in currency $100 billion.

In another sense, a trader may act in a way that is perceived as insider trading in traditional economies. For example, the merchant finds that the BOJ plans to raise rates at its next meeting from a client familiar with the governor of the Bank of Japan; the trader is free to buy as much of the yen as possible. In FX–European economic data, such as German employment stats, nothing like insider trading is often attracted days before formal publishing.

Before we let you think that FX is the world's largest and most liquid industry, note that it is the world's largest industry. It operates 24 hours a day, beginning at 5 p.m. EST on Sunday until 16:00. EST Friday and price differences are uncommon. Its magnitude and scope (from Asia to Europe to North America) render it the world's most inexpensive currency market.

2. What Is the Forex Commission?

Investors who trade in inventory, futures, or alternatives generally use a broker who acts as a broker. The broker positions the request and attempts to interchange it with the customer's commands. The officer shall carry a premium when the customer buys and transfers the tradable machine for the distribution of this product.

No transfers are made in the FX sector. FX is a major industry, contrary to overseas loan economies. FX firms are retailers, not brokers. Distributors, unlike brokers, bring business danger to investment companies through counterparties. They are not paying commission; instead, they are paying commission through the offer distribution.

In FX, the investor can not attempt to purchase on the stock or sell on an offer, as is the situation with swap economies. On the other hand, after the price clears the spread cost, there will be no additional charges or commissions. For every single penny gained, the investor is a pure profit. However, scalping in FX is much harder, as traders must always conquer the offer / work allocation.

3. What Is a Pip?

The pip is the smallest increase in FX trade and constitutes a point-in-point percentage. On the FX industry, prices are quoted for the fourth decimal stage. For example, if the soap bar in the drugstore was priced at $1.20, the same soap bar on the FX market is rated at 1.2000. The fourth digit level is 1 funnel and is typically 1/100th of 1%. The Japanese yen among the major currencies is the only exception to this law. Therefore, only two decimal points are drawn in the USD / JPY couple (i.e., 1/100th of USD, compared to 1/1000th of other major currencies).

4. What Are You Really Trading?

Nothing's the short answer. The FX retail industry is just a speculative market. There is never any swap of physical currency. All companies occur only as software requests and are networked on the basis of business costs. All gains or loses for dollar-denominated transactions are calculated in euros and recorded as such on the bill of a trader.

The primary cause for saving one currency for multinationals that need to trade currencies on an ongoing basis (i.e., wage compensation, compensation for products and facilities from foreign providers and mergers and acquisitions) is the presence of the FX industry. However, these regular company requirements create up only about 20% of the quantity of the market. Eighty percent of foreign exchange trades are of a speculation sort conducted out by significant financial organizations, hedge funds for several trillion USD, and individuals who desire to express their views on today's economic or geopolitical events.

Because currencies are always in pair trade, when a trader makes a trade, the trader is always close and brief of the other cash. For example, if a trader sold a standard EUR / USD batch (equivalent to 100,000 units), he'd exchange euros for dollars and have short and long euros now. That wasn't going to happen. An individual buying a laptop from an electronics store for $1,000 switches dollars for a computer to deeper understand this trend. For a short $1,000 and long, the person is only one computer. The store is $1,000 in length, but now there's one laptop in inventory. The FX sector, except that there is no physical exchange, is subordinate to the same values. Although all operations are submissions to the laptop, they have no less real consequences.

5. What Currencies Trade in Forex?
While some distributors are trading unusual goods like Thai Baht or Czech Coruna, most distributors are trading the seven most fluid exchange pairs in the world–the four "races":

EUR/USD (euro/dollar)

USD/JPY (dollar/Japanese yen)

GBP/USD (British pound/dollar)

USD/CHF (dollar/Swiss franc)

and the three commodity pairs:

AUD/USD (Australian dollar/dollar)

USD/CAD (dollar/Canadian dollar)

NZD/USD (New Zealand dollar/dollar)

Together with their distinct combinations–for instance, EUR / JPY, GBP / JPY, and EUR / GBP–these monetary pairs make up more than 95% of FX financial trading. With only 18 pairs or bridges traded openly, due to the restricted quantity of trading instruments, the FX industry is much higher than the stock market.

6. What Is a Currency Carry Trade?

Carry is both the largest hedge fund and the monetary exchanges ' smallest retail speculators. Carriage is focused on the reality that each currency around the world has an associated interest. These short-term interest rates are set by the U.S. Federal Reserve, the Bank of Japan in Japan, and the Bank of England in the UK.

The concept of the wagon is easy. The retailer is lengthy on currency and funds at high-interest rates, with currency at small interest rates. For instance, the NZD / JPY cross was one of the best combinations in 2005. New Zealand's economy has seen its levels rise to and stay at 7.15 percent, fueled by China's enormous supply for an item and a hot housing market. A long-time trader from NZD / JPY would have gathered 725 base points on his own. The NZD / JPY carrying company could have accomplished an initial yield of 72.5 percent on interest rate variations on the leverage of 10:1, without any input to capital appreciation. This example demonstrates why the transport sector is so common.

Before the next elevated return couple is hunted out, however, it must be advised that the declines may be rapid and severe when the airlines' trade is unwound. This method is regarded as currency trade liquidation and occurs when most speculators consider that trade with currency may have no capacity for the future. Offers are wasted for every trader who seeks to quit his role at once, and interest rate differential profits are almost insufficient to offset for capital loss. To achieve this, predicting is crucial: the best time to place the carriage is to allow the trader to travel as the price variations rise at the beginning of the price closure process.

CONCLUSION

Trading Forex, a market participant should first of all outline whether or not high or low volatility can work best with their trading vogue. If value action is additionally vital, trading, the session overlaps, or simply standard economic unleash times could be the desirable possibility. The subsequent step would be to determine what the simplest Forex trading hours or times to trade are given the bias for volatility. Those wanting high volatility can establish which era frames are most active for the currency try they're about to trade on.

When considering the EUR/USD try, the European/North American session crossover can notice the foremost movement. If a market participant from U. S. prefers to trade the active Forex open hours for GBP/JPY, for instance, they're going to have to be compelled to awaken early within the morning to stay up with the market.

If this person additionally features a regular day job, this might cause appreciable exhaustion and mistakes in terms of judgment once trading. A way bigger various for this bargainer could be trading throughout the European/North American session overlap, wherever volatility continues to be high. To boot, a good deal of information on the way to trade throughout the Forex best trading hours, doubled with a basic understanding of FX trading sessions generally, will give you a plus in terms of trading currencies properly.

Do not go yet; One last thing to do

If you enjoyed this book or found it useful, I'd be very grateful if you'd post a short review on it. Your support does make a difference, and I read all the reviews personally so I can get your feedback and make this book even better.

Thanks again for your support!